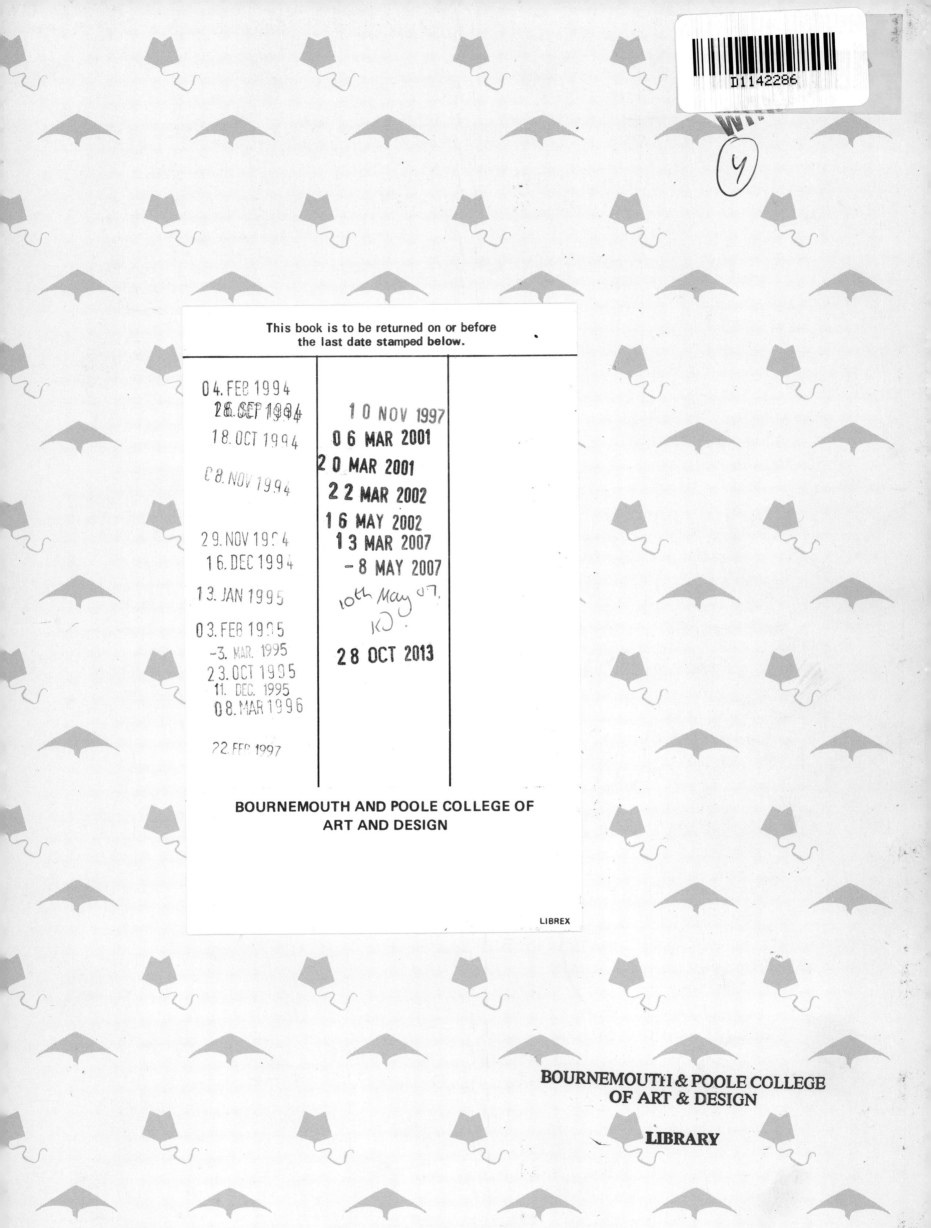

THE BOOK OF
KITES

THE BOOK OF
KITES

PAUL AND HELENE MORGAN

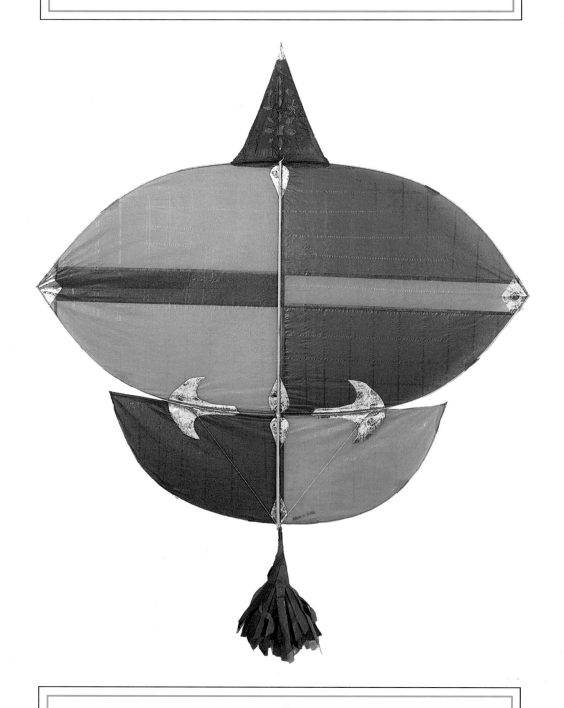

DK

DORLING KINDERSLEY
LONDON • NEW YORK • STUTTGART

A DORLING KINDERSLEY BOOK

Project editor
Tanya Hines

Design
Nigel Osborne Associates

Senior managing editor
Daphne Razazan

Managing art editor
Carole Ash

Production
Helen Creeke

First published in Great Britain in 1992
by Dorling Kindersley Limited,
9 Henrietta Street, London WC2E 8PS

A CIP catalogue record for this book is available from the British Library.

ISBN 0-86318-785-4

Reproduced in Singapore by Colourscan
Printed and bound in Italy by New Interlitho

CONTENTS

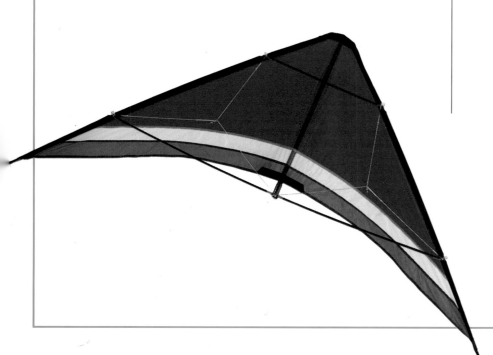

INTRODUCTION

With an ever-increasing number of kites on the market, from simple flat and bowed kites to geometric aerial sculptures and high-tech stunters, kite-flying is entering a new era of popularity. The perfect 'green' hobby, it can be practised by anyone, young or old, in town or countryside.

Kite-flying opens up a variety of experiences. The very young love the excitement of flying a small kite for the first time, and seeing it dart around in the wind, with its tail making shapes in the sky. For the older flyer, watching a large, heavy box kite flying overhead in almost total silence can be very relaxing and peaceful. In contrast, controlling a stunter in a complex series of manoeuvres can provide an exhilarating challenge as the flyer tries to match his skills against the wind.

We became involved in kite-flying through buying a plastic octopus kite at the beach for our young son Jonathan. The kite stayed up all day and we were reluctant to bring it down. The next day, we bought another kite, of a slightly different design. From then on, we were hooked. We found as many books as we could about the subject and, following the patterns in the books, began to make our first kites. The instructions were not always clear, so initially we made mistakes, but we soon got a lot of pleasure out of successfully making and flying our own kites. Becoming more adventurous, we altered the patterns to see how this affected the way that the kites flew. Before long, we were seeing potential kite shapes in everything, and had created several kites that we had taken through from initial concept to finished kite.

At this time, we decided that the hobby might just pay for itself, so with the encouragement of the local kite group, we approached a bank and in 1986 started in business as Morgan Kites. At first, we made a small range of kites: some our exclusive designs, others classics, but since then, we have gone from strength to strength and now sell our kites worldwide. We have included patterns for some of our own designs in the book.

Our most recent venture has been to set up a shop of our own, called Sky Bums, where we sell kites from many different countries, as well as specializing in our own high-quality, high-performance kites. We still derive the same thrills and enjoyment from making kites as in the early days, especially when we create one-off designs or special kites. We hope that your enthusiasm for kites and kite-flying will be fired from reading this book: it is always extremely satisfying to win over new converts to kiting.

Paul Morgan

Helene Morgan

A HISTORY OF KITES

The fascinating story of kites begins in the Far East, where they were first flown some two and a half thousand years ago. The earliest kites were often bird shaped and came to be steeped in symbolic significance. This tradition persists today in the Orient, where kites still play a central role in local folklore and legend. Kites spread to the West as trade proliferated during the Age of Discovery. Gradually their power as a flying instrument was recognized and exploited, reaching a crescendo of innovative uses in the nineteenth century.

KITES IN THE EAST

Although the precise origins of kites are lost in legend, the first recorded reference comes from China in about 500 BC, when a craftsman built what was probably a wooden bird kite. The early Chinese kites were magnificent constructions of silk and bamboo, but with the introduction of cheap paper around the second century AD, the kite became more widely available; many festivals and games based on kite-flying were born.

Traditional Chinese kites
Highly decorative kites have been flown for centuries in China and have great symbolic significance.

Japanese New Year
A lively New Year's Day street scene in Tokyo, where the exuberance of traditional dress is matched by the ornate paper kites being flown. Mount Fuji is in the background.

Military exploits

In China and Japan, the military were quick to recognize the potential of kite-power, and many of the earliest references to kites concern their military uses. Around 200 BC, a Chinese general is credited with using a kite to estimate the distance between his forces and the walls of an enemy castle, so that he could construct a tunnel of the correct length.

At about the same time, another general attached humming devices to kites, which were then flown over his enemies at night, making them think that they were being attacked by evil spirits. Ancient Japanese prints show large kites carrying archers who fired down on their enemies.

Festivals and traditions

Throughout the Far East, kite-flying has a long association with religious practice. It formed a central role in many fertility rites and ceremonies to celebrate the birth of a child, as well as festivals to invoke benign weather or rich harvests. Ancient religious writings from India relate stories of gods and goddesses taking part in kite-fighting contests. In Indonesia, kites were regarded as messengers of the gods, and were believed to represent the soul of the person who flew them.

From China, the kite was probably taken to Korea and Japan by Buddhist missionaries. At the beginning of each year, Korean families inscribe kites with the names and birthdates of all their male children, then fly the kites and release them in the belief that they take with them any evil spirits that might have plagued the children. To pick up such a kite is to take on these evil spirits.

Traditional Japanese kites are decorated with legendary characters or good luck symbols such as the dragon, which symbolizes prosperity, or the crane or tortoise, which represents long life. On the fifth day of the fifth month, Japanese families celebrate the birth of any sons during the past year by flying brightly coloured wind-inflated tubes, or windsocks, in the shape of fish.

Thailand, too, has a great tradition of flying and fighting kites. The two traditional designs are the male Chula, a large star-shaped kite, and the female Pakpao, which is a smaller diamond-shaped kite. They are flown during the monsoon to blow the rains away, and at other times of the year are used in fighting competitions, where teams of men try to entangle the kites of their opponents. Fighting kites are also popular in India, where huge crowds regularly converge for massive contests.

KITES IN THE WEST

In Europe, windsocks had been flown since Roman times, and these were possibly the forerunner of kites. Kites themselves may well have been introduced to the West in the fifteenth and sixteenth centuries by Dutch, Portuguese and English merchants trading in Far Eastern countries.

Among the earliest records of kites in Europe is a description, dated 1589, by a man named della Porta, of a rectangular kite from China, which he suggested could be used for lifting lanterns, fireworks, or even animals.

By the early eighteenth century, kites were widespread in Europe, but were seen mainly as a children's toy. Kite-fighting became an obsession in France, though, and in 1736 the sport was banned because of riot and crop damage.

The kite as a research tool

Towards the mid-eighteenth century, people began exploring the possibilities opened up by the ability to control an object in flight. Two Scotsmen, Thomas Melvill and Alexander Wilson, conducted an experiment to measure temperature variations at different altitudes. They flew six kites, with thermometers attached, in a train to a height of 900 m (3,000 ft).

Perhaps the most famous, and foolhardy, piece of research was that by Benjamin Franklin in 1752, who set out to prove that lightning was the same as generated electricity and not the wrath of God, and lofted a kite in a storm.

Pulling power

It had long been noted that a kite, once stable in flight, generated a strong pull on the line. This property was exploited to greater effect during the last century. In 1826 an Englishman, George Pocock, patented a design to use two or more large kites to pull a lightweight carriage, the *char-volant,* or flying chariot.

Others took up the idea, and by the end of the century, kites had been used for a number of different tasks, from pulling torpedoes on to their targets to drawing a cable across a gorge on the Niagara River.

Kites and electricity
Benjamin Franklin, conducting an experiment to prove the electrical nature of lightning. As the kite became wet, it conducted electricity down the line to a key. Franklin held the line by a ribbon and when he moved his knuckles towards the key, noted electrical discharges.

Man-lifting kites

The West's obsession with manned flight drew people to experiment with kites. Investigators were winched up on the kite line, using large, stable kites to provide the lift. American S.F. Cody is perhaps the name best associated with man-lifting kites (see right).

From kite to glider

In 1804, Sir George Cayley built a model glider that incorporated a kite as its main wing. He went on to build a glider that flew his coachman across a valley - the first recorded glider flight. At the end of the century, a German, Otto Lilienthal, built a kite with a wing shape like a bird's. Another pioneer, Octave Chanute, developed Lilienthal's work and designed a biplane hang-glider which helped in the experiments of the Wright brothers in America. They constructed biplane kites and larger gliders, leading to the development of the first aeroplane in December 1903.

High-tech kites

Around the turn of the century, kite design was rushing forwards. In 1893, an English emigrant in Australia, Lawrence Hargrave, perfected his two-celled box kite, used in weather forecasting. He also developed a soaring kite with a curved wing section for greater lift. American William Eddy was another major contributor to kite development. He invented his now famous bowed kite, stable in flight without a tail.

Kites were used for military observation and target practice and continued in this role even after the invention of aircraft. During the Second World War, kites were used to protect shipping.

After the war came another surge in development with the invention of non-rigid kites that relied on the wind for shape. Among these flexible kites was the sled, designed by William Allison in America.

In 1963, American Domina Jalbert hit upon the idea of the Parafoil kite based on an aeroplane wing section. A few years later, the highly manoeuvrable Flexifoil was invented, and soon after that, Peter Powell's stunt kite came on to the market, heralding the beginning of a new era of popular interest in kite-flying.

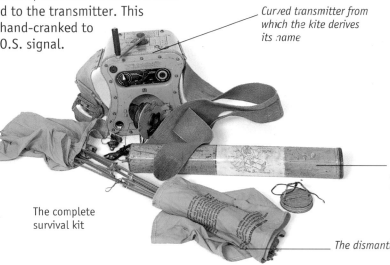

S.F. Cody being lofted by his famous winged box kite.

Saved by a kite

At the end of the last century, a Frenchman, C. Jobert, devised a system for rescuing shipwrecked sailors. Taking advantage of strong winds that tended to accompany shipping disasters, he would fly a kite with a rope attached that could be reached by those on ship, who were then winched to safety.

FLAMBOYANT CODY

One of the most colourful of kiting pioneers is surely Samuel Franklin Cody, an American who settled in England. In 1901, he patented a winged version of a double-celled box kite, which was used for man-lifting. Other exploits included a kite-powered crossing of the English Channel. Despite his keenness to put his inventions to practical use, he was not taken seriously by the military: his long hair and Wild West show made him too unconventional. However, in 1906, he was given officer status at Farnborough, England, where he built the Cody war kites. He was also the first man in Britain to fly an aeroplane. He met his death in 1913 when another of his creations broke up in flight.

The Gibson Girl

Perhaps the most famous kite of the Second World War, the Gibson Girl was so-called because of the waist-like shape of its accompanying radio transmitter. The kite was part of a survival kit for airmen whose plane had crashed into the sea, and was flown on a thin aerial, attached to the transmitter. This could then be hand-cranked to send out an S.O.S. signal.

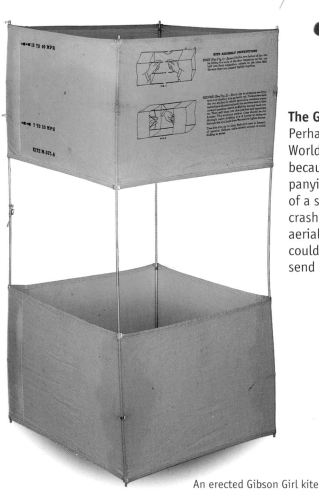

An erected Gibson Girl kite

Curved transmitter from which the kite derives its name

Durable metal case for storing the kite

The complete survival kit

The dismantled kite

A CATALOGUE OF KITES

To introduce you to the enormous diversity of kite designs available today, here is a selection of classic and high-tech kites from all over the world, arranged by type of kite.

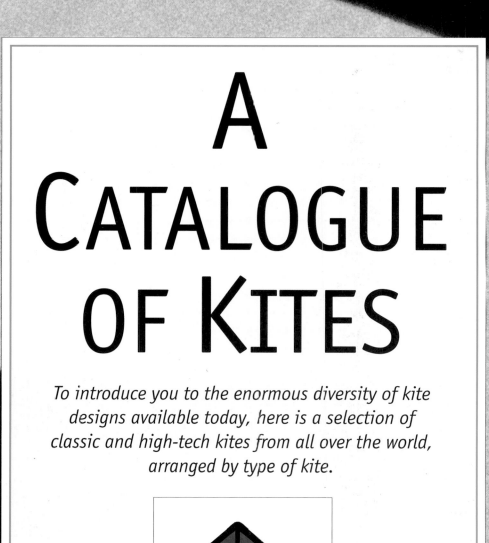

ANATOMY OF A KITE

Although kite designs vary enormously, kites have a number of basic features and components in common in terms of their framework and construction. The three kites shown below - a soft kite, a stunter and a box kite - provide a visual glossary exemplifying the key features of kite anatomy, from the leading edge to individual cells.

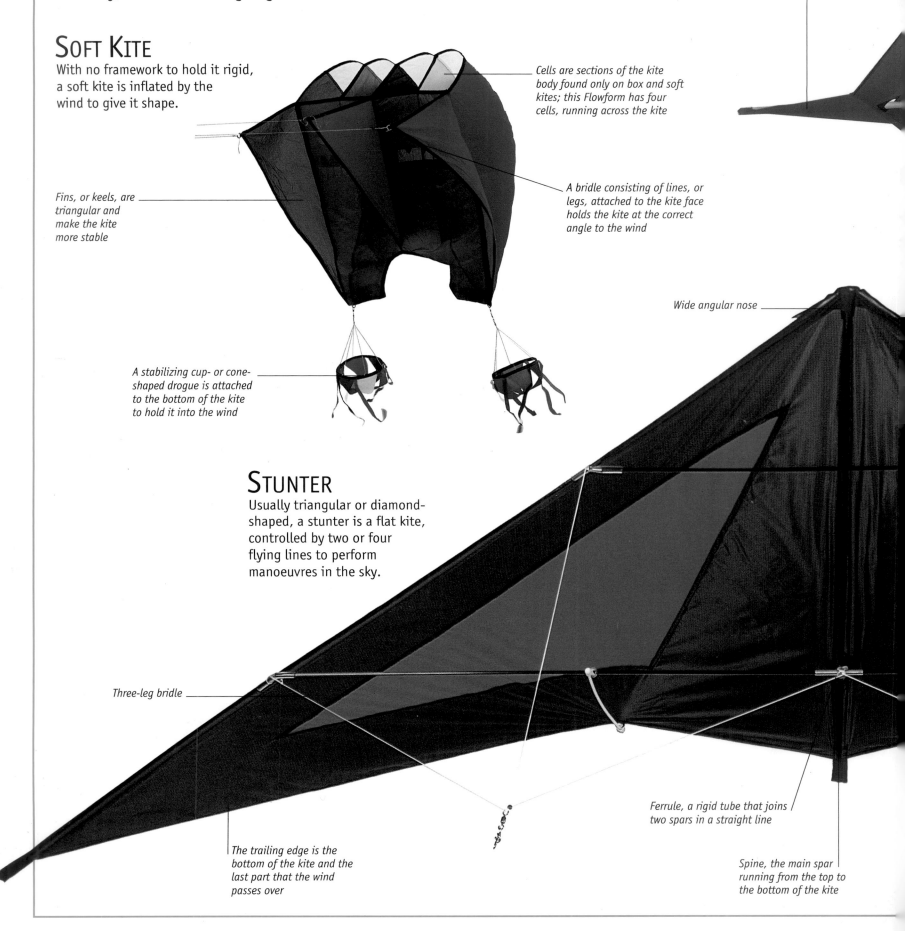

SOFT KITE

With no framework to hold it rigid, a soft kite is inflated by the wind to give it shape.

Jibs, small wings that allow the spars to be attached to the cover outside the main body of the kite so that tension is spread evenly throughout

Cells are sections of the kite body found only on box and soft kites; this Flowform has four cells, running across the kite

Fins, or keels, are triangular and make the kite more stable

A bridle consisting of lines, or legs, attached to the kite face holds the kite at the correct angle to the wind

A stabilizing cup- or cone-shaped drogue is attached to the bottom of the kite to hold it into the wind

Wide angular nose

STUNTER

Usually triangular or diamond-shaped, a stunter is a flat kite, controlled by two or four flying lines to perform manoeuvres in the sky.

Three-leg bridle

Ferrule, a rigid tube that joins two spars in a straight line

The trailing edge is the bottom of the kite and the last part that the wind passes over

Spine, the main spar running from the top to the bottom of the kite

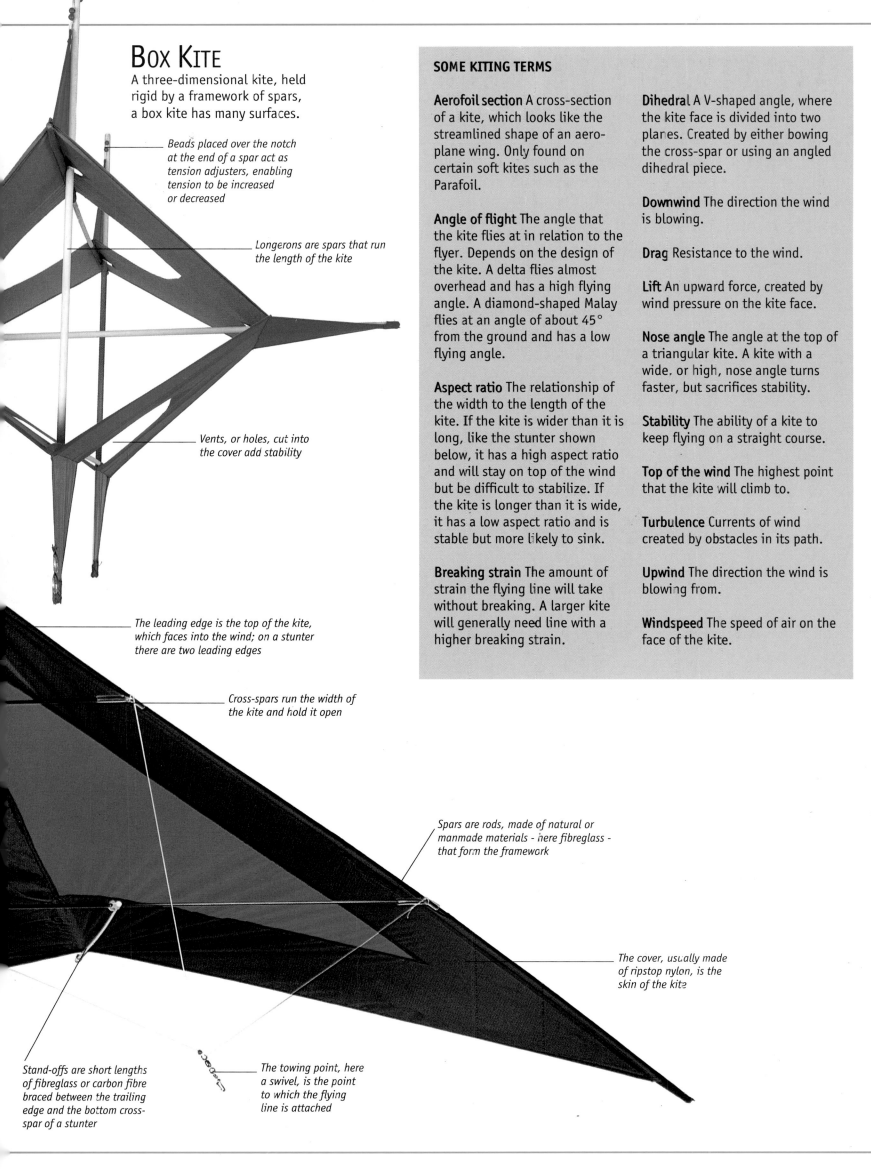

BOX KITE

A three-dimensional kite, held rigid by a framework of spars, a box kite has many surfaces.

Beads placed over the notch at the end of a spar act as tension adjusters, enabling tension to be increased or decreased

Longerons are spars that run the length of the kite

Vents, or holes, cut into the cover add stability

The leading edge is the top of the kite, which faces into the wind; on a stunter there are two leading edges

Cross-spars run the width of the kite and hold it open

Spars are rods, made of natural or manmade materials - here fibreglass - that form the framework

The cover, usually made of ripstop nylon, is the skin of the kite

Stand-offs are short lengths of fibreglass or carbon fibre braced between the trailing edge and the bottom cross-spar of a stunter

The towing point, here a swivel, is the point to which the flying line is attached

SOME KITING TERMS

Aerofoil section A cross-section of a kite, which looks like the streamlined shape of an aeroplane wing. Only found on certain soft kites such as the Parafoil.

Angle of flight The angle that the kite flies at in relation to the flyer. Depends on the design of the kite. A delta flies almost overhead and has a high flying angle. A diamond-shaped Malay flies at an angle of about 45° from the ground and has a low flying angle.

Aspect ratio The relationship of the width to the length of the kite. If the kite is wider than it is long, like the stunter shown below, it has a high aspect ratio and will stay on top of the wind but be difficult to stabilize. If the kite is longer than it is wide, it has a low aspect ratio and is stable but more likely to sink.

Breaking strain The amount of strain the flying line will take without breaking. A larger kite will generally need line with a higher breaking strain.

Dihedral A V-shaped angle, where the kite face is divided into two planes. Created by either bowing the cross-spar or using an angled dihedral piece.

Downwind The direction the wind is blowing.

Drag Resistance to the wind.

Lift An upward force, created by wind pressure on the kite face.

Nose angle The angle at the top of a triangular kite. A kite with a wide, or high, nose angle turns faster, but sacrifices stability.

Stability The ability of a kite to keep flying on a straight course.

Top of the wind The highest point that the kite will climb to.

Turbulence Currents of wind created by obstacles in its path.

Upwind The direction the wind is blowing from.

Windspeed The speed of air on the face of the kite.

TRADITIONAL KITES

O ften highly decorative and emblazoned with drag-
ons, serpents and other legendary creatures or
characters, traditional kites are flown in festivals all
over the world. Many come from the Far East, where
kite-flying can be traced back for thousands of years.
Some, such as the Chinese centipede, are almost exact
copies of the original design; others are a variation,
where perhaps modern materials have been used in the
construction, or the face of the kite made more decorative. Traditional kites are exported to the West,
although the cheaper mass-produced versions are
mainly used for ornament, being fragile and not
as accurately made as those manufactured in small
numbers or as special one-off designs.

Japanese Edo
An accurate miniature
version of a classic Japanese design, with a paper
cover printed in traditional style
and a split bamboo frame. The
kite is flown bowed, but because of its size it is stable in
only the lightest of winds.

Size
6 x 8.5 cm (2½ x 3½ in)
Wind strength
Very light
Level of skill
Intermediate to
advanced
Line
1-2 kg (2-4½ lb)

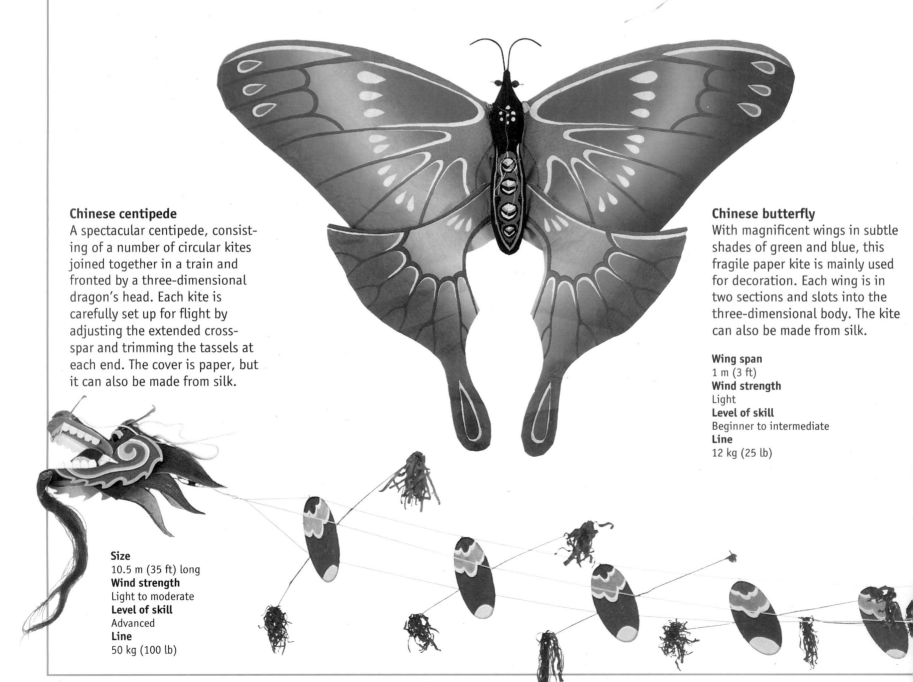

Chinese centipede
A spectacular centipede, consisting of a number of circular kites
joined together in a train and
fronted by a three-dimensional
dragon's head. Each kite is
carefully set up for flight by
adjusting the extended cross-
spar and trimming the tassels at
each end. The cover is paper, but
it can also be made from silk.

Size
10.5 m (35 ft) long
Wind strength
Light to moderate
Level of skill
Advanced
Line
50 kg (100 lb)

Chinese butterfly
With magnificent wings in subtle
shades of green and blue, this
fragile paper kite is mainly used
for decoration. Each wing is in
two sections and slots into the
three-dimensional body. The kite
can also be made from silk.

Wing span
1 m (3 ft)
Wind strength
Light
Level of skill
Beginner to intermediate
Line
12 kg (25 lb)

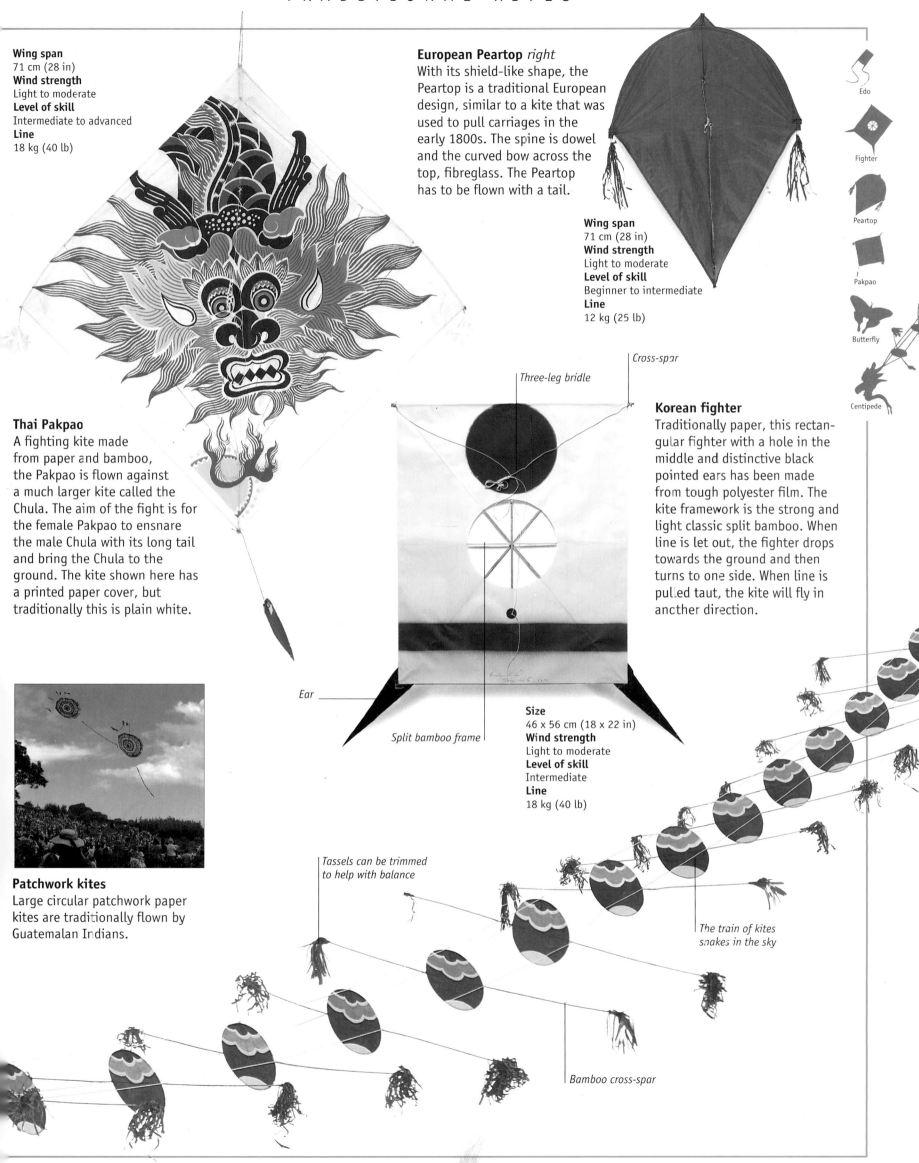

Wing span
71 cm (28 in)
Wind strength
Light to moderate
Level of skill
Intermediate to advanced
Line
18 kg (40 lb)

European Peartop *right*
With its shield-like shape, the Peartop is a traditional European design, similar to a kite that was used to pull carriages in the early 1800s. The spine is dowel and the curved bow across the top, fibreglass. The Peartop has to be flown with a tail.

Wing span
71 cm (28 in)
Wind strength
Light to moderate
Level of skill
Beginner to intermediate
Line
12 kg (25 lb)

Edo

Fighter

Peartop

Pakpao

Butterfly

Centipede

Cross-spar

Three-leg bridle

Korean fighter
Traditionally paper, this rectangular fighter with a hole in the middle and distinctive black pointed ears has been made from tough polyester film. The kite framework is the strong and light classic split bamboo. When line is let out, the fighter drops towards the ground and then turns to one side. When line is pulled taut, the kite will fly in another direction.

Ear

Split bamboo frame

Size
46 x 56 cm (18 x 22 in)
Wind strength
Light to moderate
Level of skill
Intermediate
Line
18 kg (40 lb)

Thai Pakpao
A fighting kite made from paper and bamboo, the Pakpao is flown against a much larger kite called the Chula. The aim of the fight is for the female Pakpao to ensnare the male Chula with its long tail and bring the Chula to the ground. The kite shown here has a printed paper cover, but traditionally this is plain white.

Patchwork kites
Large circular patchwork paper kites are traditionally flown by Guatemalan Indians.

Tassels can be trimmed to help with balance

The train of kites snakes in the sky

Bamboo cross-spar

FLAT KITES

The oldest of all kites, flat kites are often very simply constructed, which leaves the face open to complex decoration. When this is coupled with a long colourful tail, the kite looks spectacular in the sky. Flat kites are inherently unstable. Without some form of added stability, they will spin and fall from the sky. One way to achieve this stability is to add a tail, which keeps the kite pointing into the wind by adding drag, or resistance, to the rear. With a tail, too, these kites will often fly in much stronger winds than many other kites. Another way of gaining stability is to use light cross-spars, which allow the wind to bow them back, creating a curved shape.

Size
1.2 m (4 ft) across
Wind strength
Moderate
Level of skill
Intermediate
Line
27 kg (60 lb)

Sode
This attractively appliquéd kite is inspired by the Japanese kimono. It has no tail but instead gains stability by three light cross-spars, which hold the face open at the top, bottom and across the middle, and give it a natural curve in flight. The spine runs down the centre.

Della Porta
A very simple rectangular kite, with two diagonal spars and a long loop tail for stability. Each end of the tail is attached to a side at the bottom of the kite. If the kite begins to turn to one side, the tail becomes effectively longer on the other side and so pulls the kite back into the wind.

Size
45 x 70 cm (17³/₄ x 27¹/₂ in)
Wind strength
Light to strong
Level of skill
Beginner
Line
12 kg (25 lb)

Loop tail

Diagonal spar

Three-leg bridle

The cover is made from paper

The tail is an integral part of the design

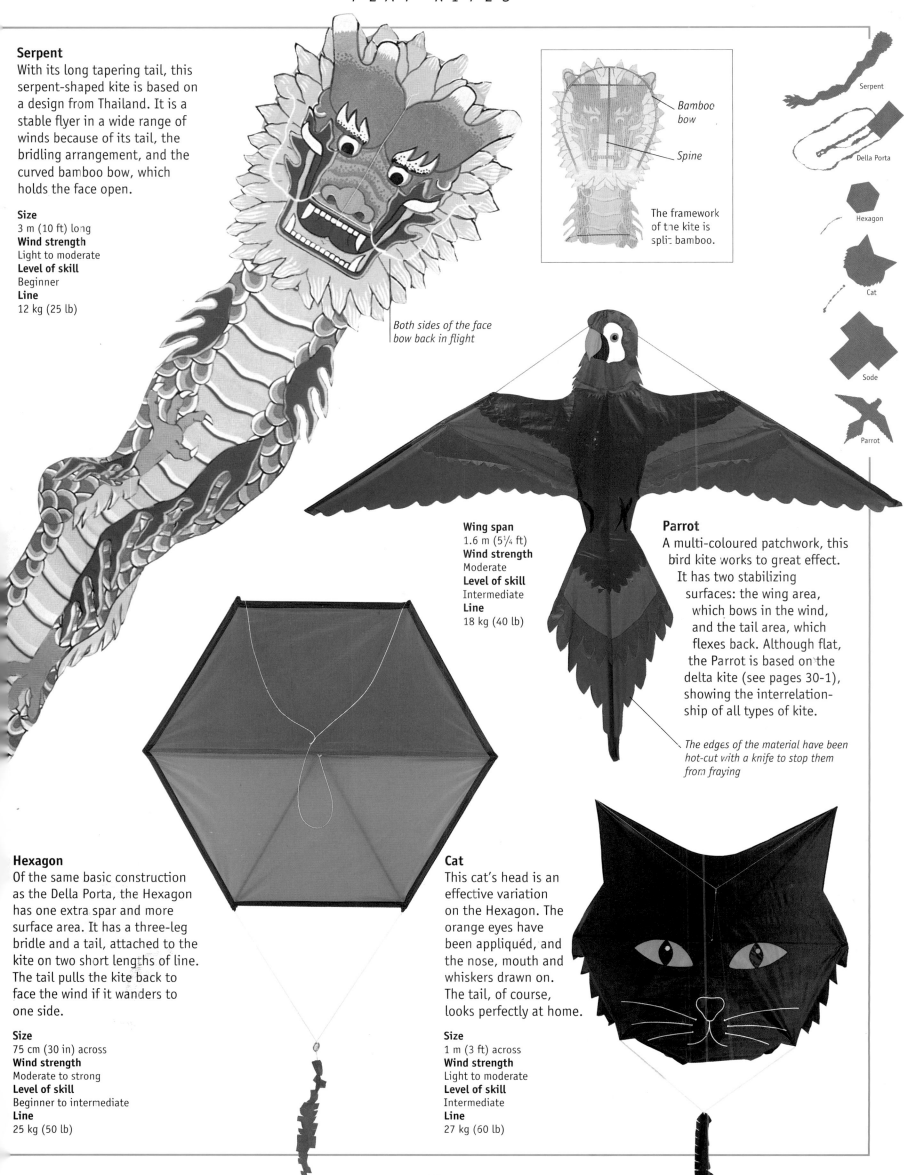

Serpent

With its long tapering tail, this serpent-shaped kite is based on a design from Thailand. It is a stable flyer in a wide range of winds because of its tail, the bridling arrangement, and the curved bamboo bow, which holds the face open.

Size
3 m (10 ft) long
Wind strength
Light to moderate
Level of skill
Beginner
Line
12 kg (25 lb)

Bamboo bow

Spine

The framework of the kite is split bamboo.

Serpent

Della Porta

Hexagon

Cat

Sode

Parrot

Both sides of the face bow back in flight

Wing span
1.6 m (5¼ ft)
Wind strength
Moderate
Level of skill
Intermediate
Line
18 kg (40 lb)

Parrot

A multi-coloured patchwork, this bird kite works to great effect. It has two stabilizing surfaces: the wing area, which bows in the wind, and the tail area, which flexes back. Although flat, the Parrot is based on the delta kite (see pages 30-1), showing the interrelationship of all types of kite.

The edges of the material have been hot-cut with a knife to stop them from fraying

Hexagon

Of the same basic construction as the Della Porta, the Hexagon has one extra spar and more surface area. It has a three-leg bridle and a tail, attached to the kite on two short lengths of line. The tail pulls the kite back to face the wind if it wanders to one side.

Size
75 cm (30 in) across
Wind strength
Moderate to strong
Level of skill
Beginner to intermediate
Line
25 kg (50 lb)

Cat

This cat's head is an effective variation on the Hexagon. The orange eyes have been appliquéd, and the nose, mouth and whiskers drawn on. The tail, of course, looks perfectly at home.

Size
1 m (3 ft) across
Wind strength
Light to moderate
Level of skill
Intermediate
Line
27 kg (60 lb)

BOWED & DIHEDRAL KITES

These kites have inbuilt stability because of the curved shape of the kite face and so are less reliant on tails than flat kites. This shape is created by either bowing the cross-spar or using an angled dihedral piece, into which the cross-spar slots. The surface of the kite is thus split into two planes. If the kite turns to one side, then that plane offers more surface area to the wind so the kite is blown back into position.

Complex six-legged bridle, allowing adjustment of the flight angle

Diamond
Otherwise known as the Malay, or Eddy bow kite, the Diamond is the classic kite-shaped kite, and is one of the most popular kites today. To give it stability, it is mostly flown bowed or with a dihedral piece, but it can be flown flat with a long tail.

Wing span
80 cm (31½ in)
Wind strength
Light to moderate
Level of skill
Beginner
Line
12 kg (25 lb)

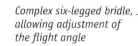

Yakko
A traditional Japanese design in modern materials, the Yakko has an appliquéd ripstop nylon face, framed by a fibreglass hoop. In flight, the wind flexes this back at the bottom and also blows through the vents on either side, making a curved shape.

Size
84 cm (33 in) across
Wind strength
Light to moderate
Level of skill
Beginner
Line
12 kg (25 lb)

Vent

Rokkaku *above*
A traditional Japanese design, the Rokkaku is very stable because of its two bowed cross-spars, and needs little attention in the sky. It has become in-creasingly popular as a fighter in competitions worldwide.

Size
1.6 x 2 m (5¼ x 6½ ft)
Wind strength
Moderate
Level of skill
Beginner to intermediate
Line
90 kg (200 lb)

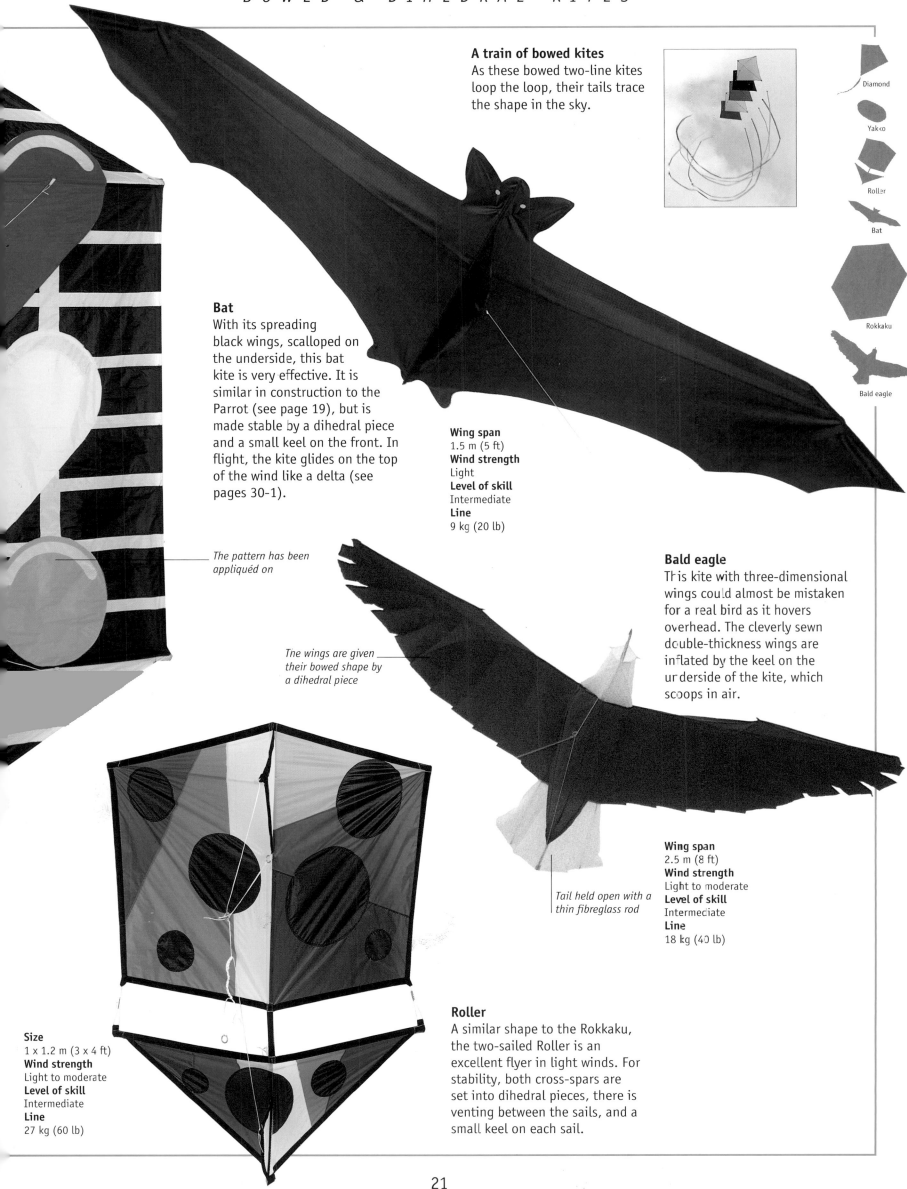

A train of bowed kites
As these bowed two-line kites loop the loop, their tails trace the shape in the sky.

Diamond

Yakko

Roller

Bat

Rokkaku

Bald eagle

Bat
With its spreading black wings, scalloped on the underside, this bat kite is very effective. It is similar in construction to the Parrot (see page 19), but is made stable by a dihedral piece and a small keel on the front. In flight, the kite glides on the top of the wind like a delta (see pages 30-1).

The pattern has been appliquéd on

Wing span
1.5 m (5 ft)
Wind strength
Light
Level of skill
Intermediate
Line
9 kg (20 lb)

Bald eagle
This kite with three-dimensional wings could almost be mistaken for a real bird as it hovers overhead. The cleverly sewn double-thickness wings are inflated by the keel on the underside of the kite, which scoops in air.

The wings are given their bowed shape by a dihedral piece

Tail held open with a thin fibreglass rod

Wing span
2.5 m (8 ft)
Wind strength
Light to moderate
Level of skill
Intermediate
Line
18 kg (40 lb)

Roller
A similar shape to the Rokkaku, the two-sailed Roller is an excellent flyer in light winds. For stability, both cross-spars are set into dihedral pieces, there is venting between the sails, and a small keel on each sail.

Size
1 x 1.2 m (3 x 4 ft)
Wind strength
Light to moderate
Level of skill
Intermediate
Line
27 kg (60 lb)

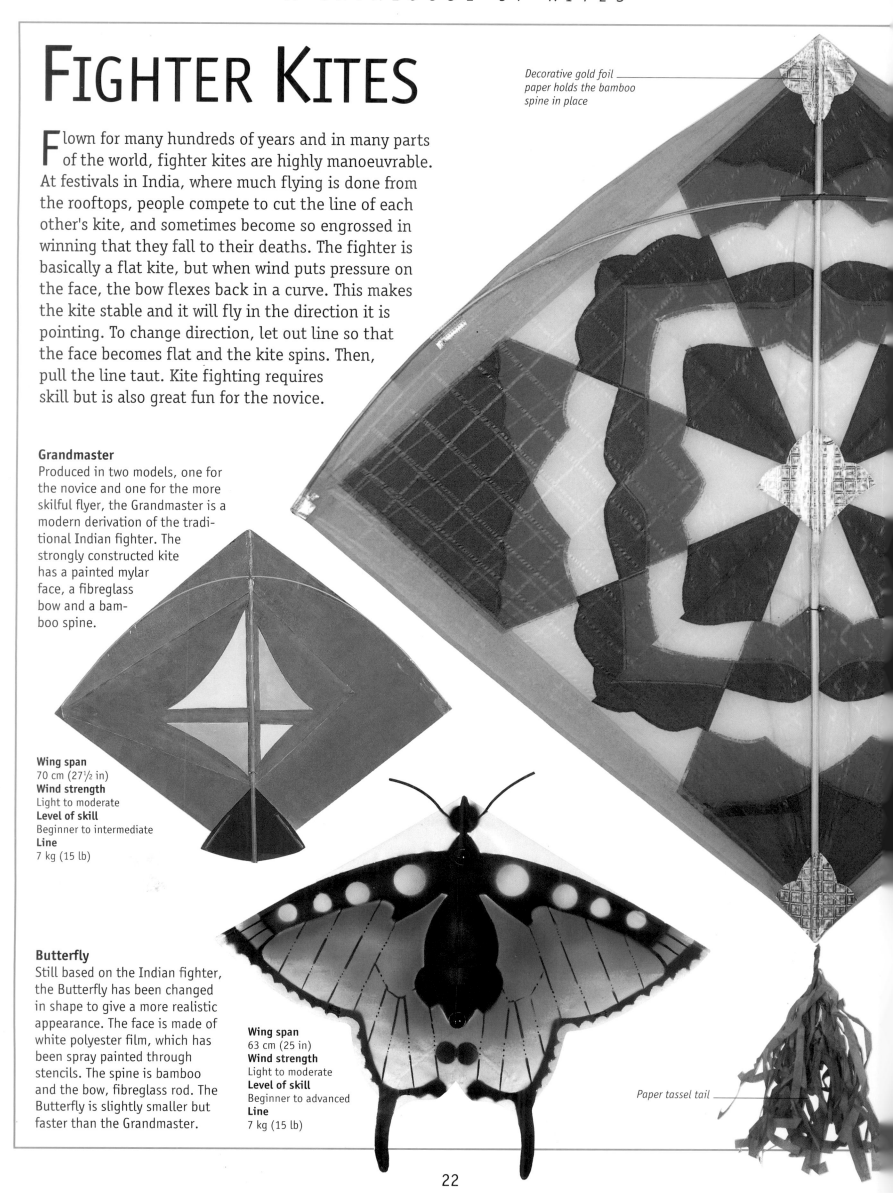

FIGHTER KITES

Flown for many hundreds of years and in many parts of the world, fighter kites are highly manoeuvrable. At festivals in India, where much flying is done from the rooftops, people compete to cut the line of each other's kite, and sometimes become so engrossed in winning that they fall to their deaths. The fighter is basically a flat kite, but when wind puts pressure on the face, the bow flexes back in a curve. This makes the kite stable and it will fly in the direction it is pointing. To change direction, let out line so that the face becomes flat and the kite spins. Then, pull the line taut. Kite fighting requires skill but is also great fun for the novice.

Decorative gold foil paper holds the bamboo spine in place

Grandmaster
Produced in two models, one for the novice and one for the more skilful flyer, the Grandmaster is a modern derivation of the traditional Indian fighter. The strongly constructed kite has a painted mylar face, a fibreglass bow and a bamboo spine.

Wing span
70 cm (27½ in)
Wind strength
Light to moderate
Level of skill
Beginner to intermediate
Line
7 kg (15 lb)

Butterfly
Still based on the Indian fighter, the Butterfly has been changed in shape to give a more realistic appearance. The face is made of white polyester film, which has been spray painted through stencils. The spine is bamboo and the bow, fibreglass rod. The Butterfly is slightly smaller but faster than the Grandmaster.

Wing span
63 cm (25 in)
Wind strength
Light to moderate
Level of skill
Beginner to advanced
Line
7 kg (15 lb)

Paper tassel tail

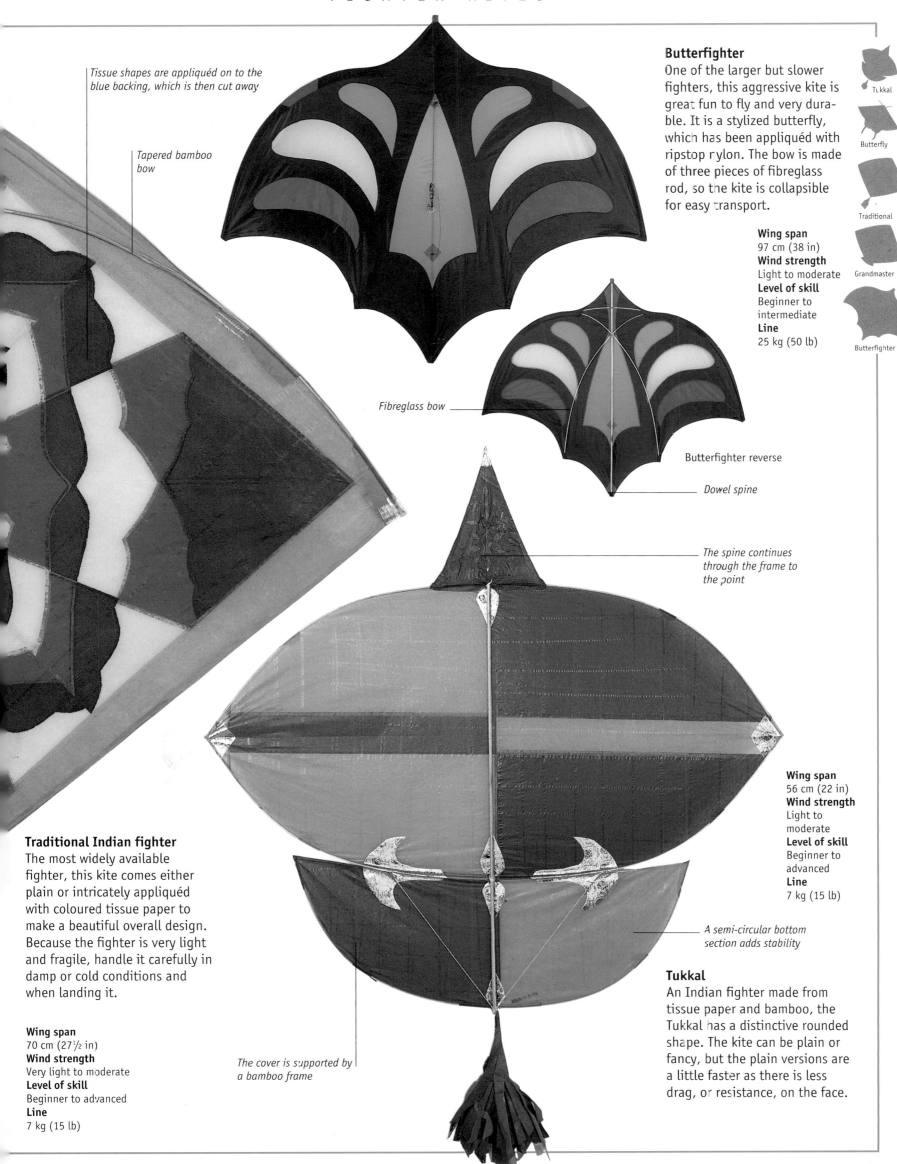

Tissue shapes are appliquéd on to the blue backing, which is then cut away

Tapered bamboo bow

Butterfighter
One of the larger but slower fighters, this aggressive kite is great fun to fly and very durable. It is a stylized butterfly, which has been appliquéd with ripstop rylon. The bow is made of three pieces of fibreglass rod, so the kite is collapsible for easy transport.

Wing span
97 cm (38 in)
Wind strength
Light to moderate
Level of skill
Beginner to intermediate
Line
25 kg (50 lb)

Tukkal

Butterfly

Traditional

Grandmaster

Butterfighter

Fibreglass bow

Butterfighter reverse

Dowel spine

The spine continues through the frame to the point

Traditional Indian fighter
The most widely available fighter, this kite comes either plain or intricately appliquéd with coloured tissue paper to make a beautiful overall design. Because the fighter is very light and fragile, handle it carefully in damp or cold conditions and when landing it.

Wing span
70 cm (27½ in)
Wind strength
Very light to moderate
Level of skill
Beginner to advanced
Line
7 kg (15 lb)

The cover is supported by a bamboo frame

Wing span
56 cm (22 in)
Wind strength
Light to moderate
Level of skill
Beginner to advanced
Line
7 kg (15 lb)

A semi-circular bottom section adds stability

Tukkal
An Indian fighter made from tissue paper and bamboo, the Tukkal has a distinctive rounded shape. The kite can be plain or fancy, but the plain versions are a little faster as there is less drag, or resistance, on the face.

BOX KITES

The multi-surfaced box kite is very stable and will fly in stronger winds than other kites. Invented at the end of the last century, it marked a major advance in kite design. Box kites have been used in biplane development, for weather forecasting, to protect shipping in the Second World War, and even to carry people. In recent years, the design of box kites has become very complex, but even these sophisticated aerial sculptures can still be traced back to the classic two-celled box.

Geometric box
A Tri-D in full flight with trailing windsocks.

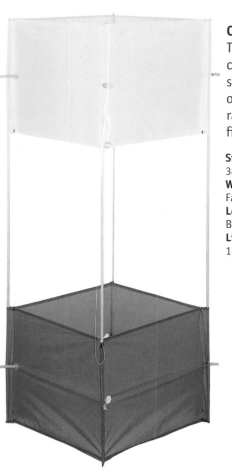

Classic box
The basic box kite has two square cells, one above the other, and serves as a prototype for most other boxes. It is stable in a wide range of winds. The cells are held firmly by a two-leg bridle.

Size
38 cm x 1 m (15 in x 3 ft)
Wind strength
Fairly light to strong
Level of skill
Beginner
Line
12 kg (25 lb)

Rhomboid
A variation on the standard two-celled box, the three-celled Rhomboid presents more area to the wind and so flies in even quite light windspeeds. Because of the small wings, or jibs, the spars pass outside the cover of the kite, putting an even tension across the whole cell.

Size
1.1 x 1.4 m (3½ x 4½ ft)
Wind strength
Light to strong
Level of skill
Intermediate
Line
25 kg (50 lb)

Spars run the full length of the kite

Cody
A stable flyer with the aesthetics of a vintage model, the Cody was designed and built early this century to be used as a manlifter for British army reconnaissance. It is still very popular today.

Wing span
1.2 m (4 ft)
Wind strength
Moderate
Level of skill
Intermediate
Line
27 kg (60 lb)

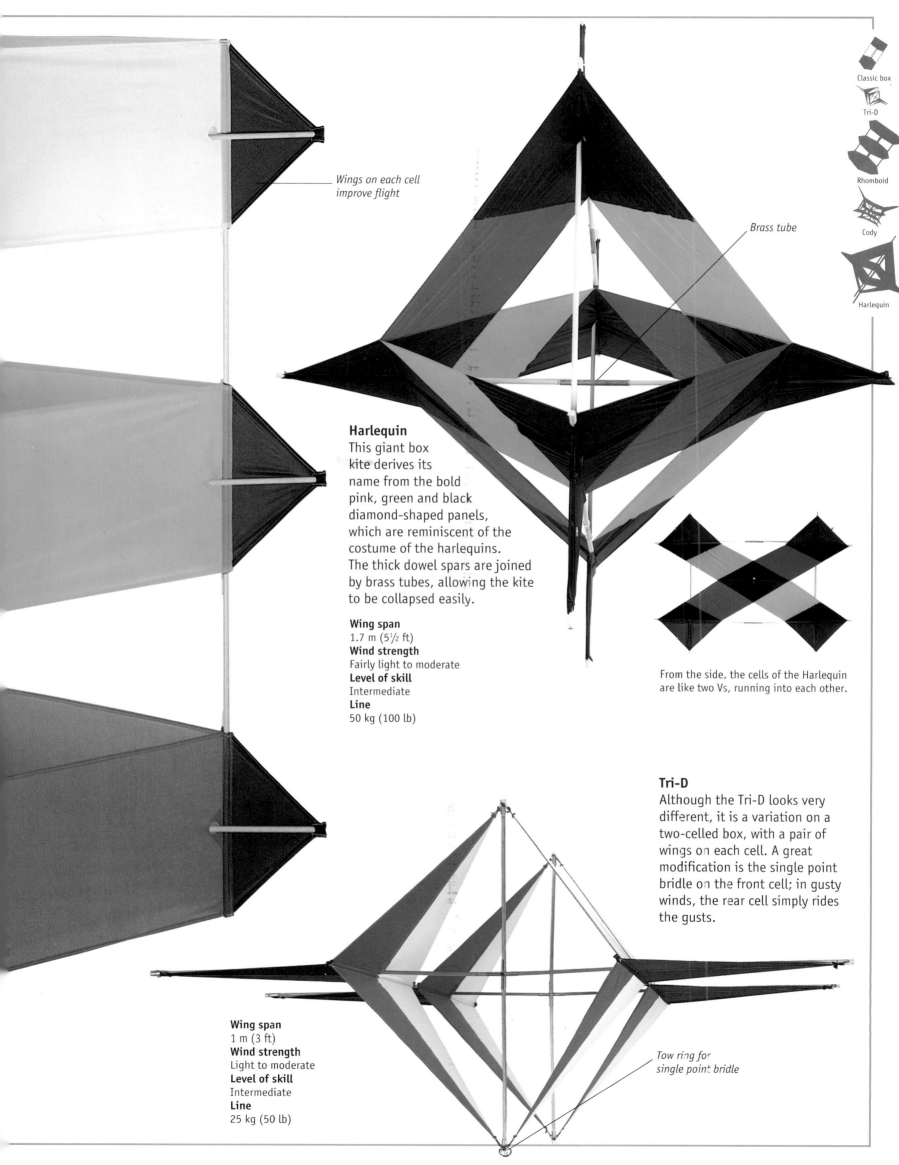

Classic box

Tri-D

Rhomboid

Cody

Harlequin

Wings on each cell improve flight

Brass tube

Harlequin

This giant box kite derives its name from the bold pink, green and black diamond-shaped panels, which are reminiscent of the costume of the harlequins. The thick dowel spars are joined by brass tubes, allowing the kite to be collapsed easily.

Wing span
1.7 m (5½ ft)
Wind strength
Fairly light to moderate
Level of skill
Intermediate
Line
50 kg (100 lb)

From the side, the cells of the Harlequin are like two Vs, running into each other.

Tri-D

Although the Tri-D looks very different, it is a variation on a two-celled box, with a pair of wings on each cell. A great modification is the single point bridle on the front cell; in gusty winds, the rear cell simply rides the gusts.

Wing span
1 m (3 ft)
Wind strength
Light to moderate
Level of skill
Intermediate
Line
25 kg (50 lb)

Tow ring for single point bridle

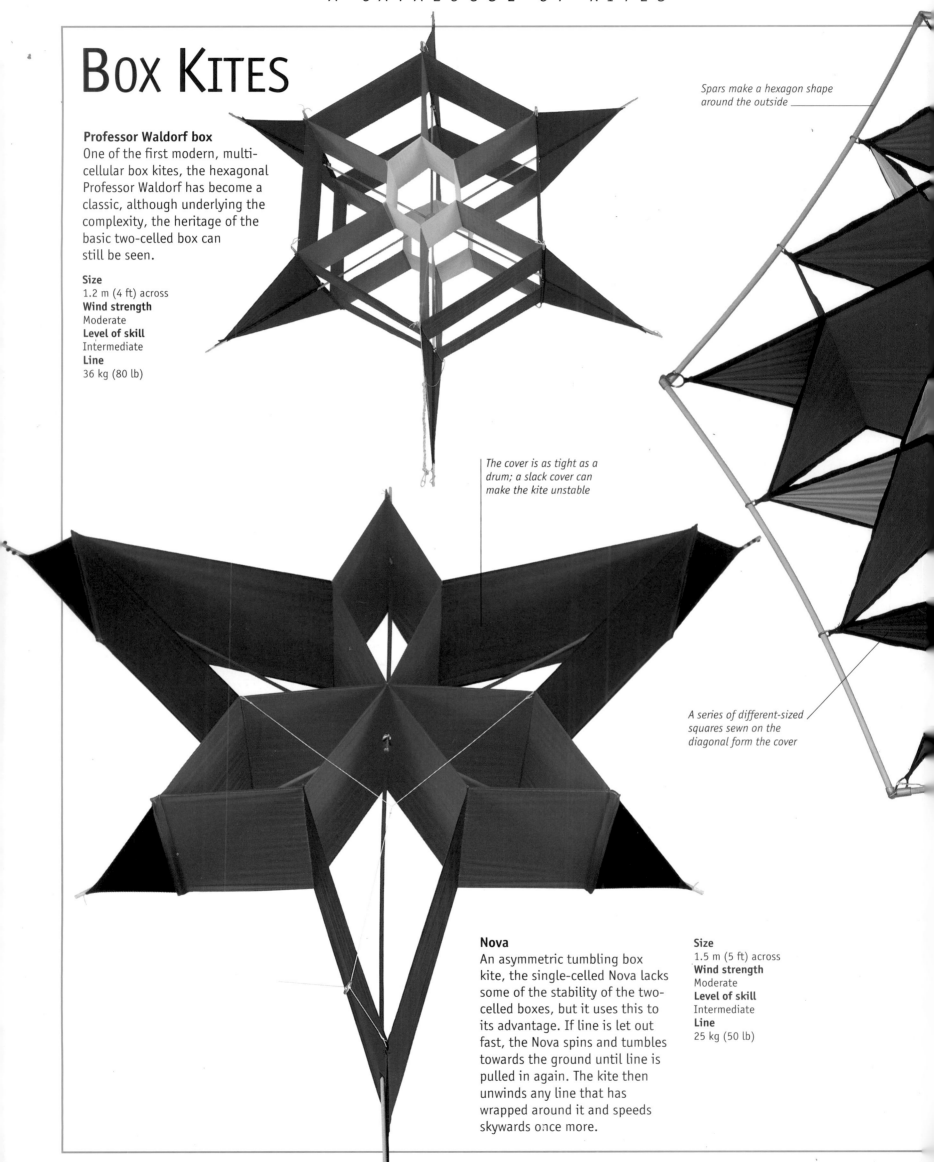

BOX KITES

Professor Waldorf box
One of the first modern, multi-cellular box kites, the hexagonal Professor Waldorf has become a classic, although underlying the complexity, the heritage of the basic two-celled box can still be seen.

Size
1.2 m (4 ft) across
Wind strength
Moderate
Level of skill
Intermediate
Line
36 kg (80 lb)

Spars make a hexagon shape around the outside

The cover is as tight as a drum; a slack cover can make the kite unstable

A series of different-sized squares sewn on the diagonal form the cover

Nova
An asymmetric tumbling box kite, the single-celled Nova lacks some of the stability of the two-celled boxes, but it uses this to its advantage. If line is let out fast, the Nova spins and tumbles towards the ground until line is pulled in again. The kite then unwinds any line that has wrapped around it and speeds skywards once more.

Size
1.5 m (5 ft) across
Wind strength
Moderate
Level of skill
Intermediate
Line
25 kg (50 lb)

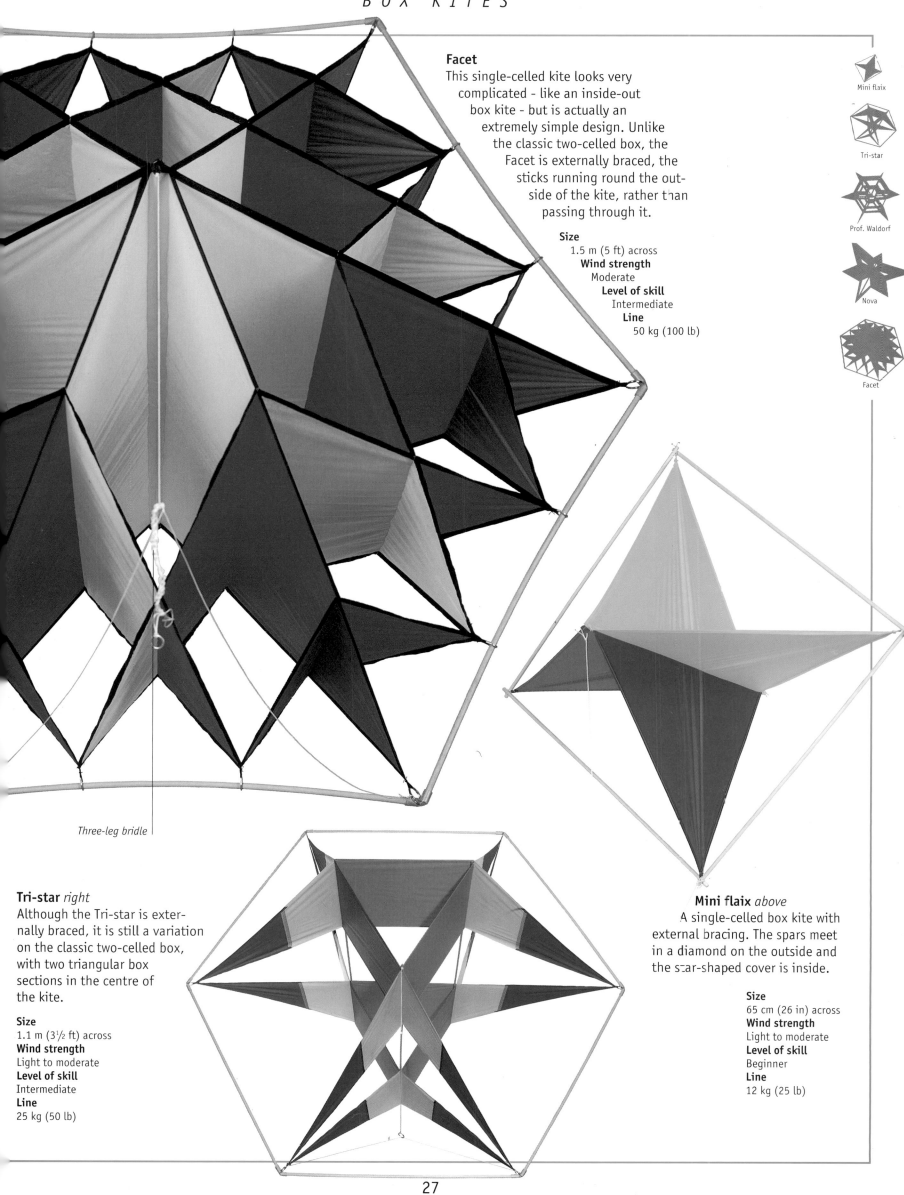

Facet
This single-celled kite looks very complicated - like an inside-out box kite - but is actually an extremely simple design. Unlike the classic two-celled box, the Facet is externally braced, the sticks running round the outside of the kite, rather than passing through it.

Size
1.5 m (5 ft) across
Wind strength
Moderate
Level of skill
Intermediate
Line
50 kg (100 lb)

Mini flaix

Tri-star

Prof. Waldorf

Nova

Facet

Three-leg bridle

Mini flaix *above*
A single-celled box kite with external bracing. The spars meet in a diamond on the outside and the star-shaped cover is inside.

Size
65 cm (26 in) across
Wind strength
Light to moderate
Level of skill
Beginner
Line
12 kg (25 lb)

Tri-star *right*
Although the Tri-star is externally braced, it is still a variation on the classic two-celled box, with two triangular box sections in the centre of the kite.

Size
1.1 m (3½ ft) across
Wind strength
Light to moderate
Level of skill
Intermediate
Line
25 kg (50 lb)

SLED KITES

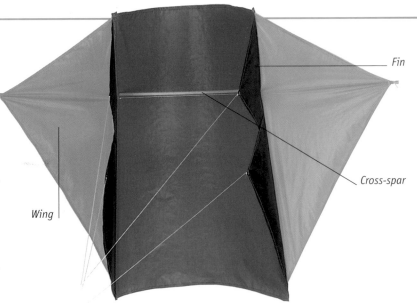

Fin

Cross-spar

Wing

When it was introduced, the flexible sled kite was quite a departure from the usual design of a kite because it is only supported along its length and relies on the wind to hold it open in flight. The basic sled was patented in the 1950s and there have been only fairly superficial alterations since then. Because of its simplicity, the sled is one of the most popular kites to make, and almost any light materials can be used in its construction: paper, ripstop nylon, even a plastic bag will serve as a cover, with spars made of dowel or perhaps drinking straws. The sled is fairly stable in flight but a cross-wind may push the sides of the kite together.

Winged sled
As well as double fins, this kite has a wing on each side and a cross-spar passing through the fins. The cross-spar is not long enough to stretch the cover taut but allows it to flex in the normal way.

Wing span
1.2 m (4 ft)
Wind strength
Moderate
Level of skill
Beginner to intermediate
Line
25 kg (50 lb)

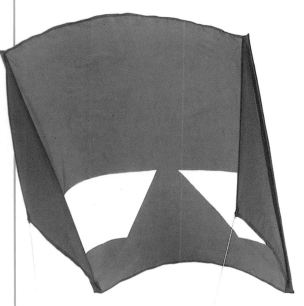

Grauel sled *left*
The basic sled had two triangular fins and no vents, but it was discovered that the kite was made more stable by cutting holes in its cover. A number of variations with vents have been tried: this one by Ed Grauel is a popular version.

Wing span
99 cm (39 in)
Wind strength
Moderate
Level of skill
Beginner to intermediate
Line
25 kg (50 lb)

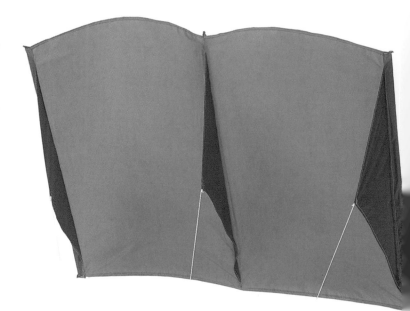

Double sled
Two sleds have been joined together to form a double sled, with an extra fin in the middle. The only problem with this design is that in cross-winds, the sides vibrate in and out, making the kite look like a concertina.

Wing span
94 cm (37 in)
Wind strength
Moderate
Level of skill
Beginner to intermediate
Line
25 kg (50 lb)

Soft sled
Very light and portable, this sled is almost indestructible. Instead of spars, the kite has a tube on each side, which is inflated by the wind, to hold the cover open in the normal way.

Wing span
50 cm (20 in)
Wind strength
Moderate
Level of skill
Beginner to intermediate
Line
25 kg (50 lb)

Trailing windsock

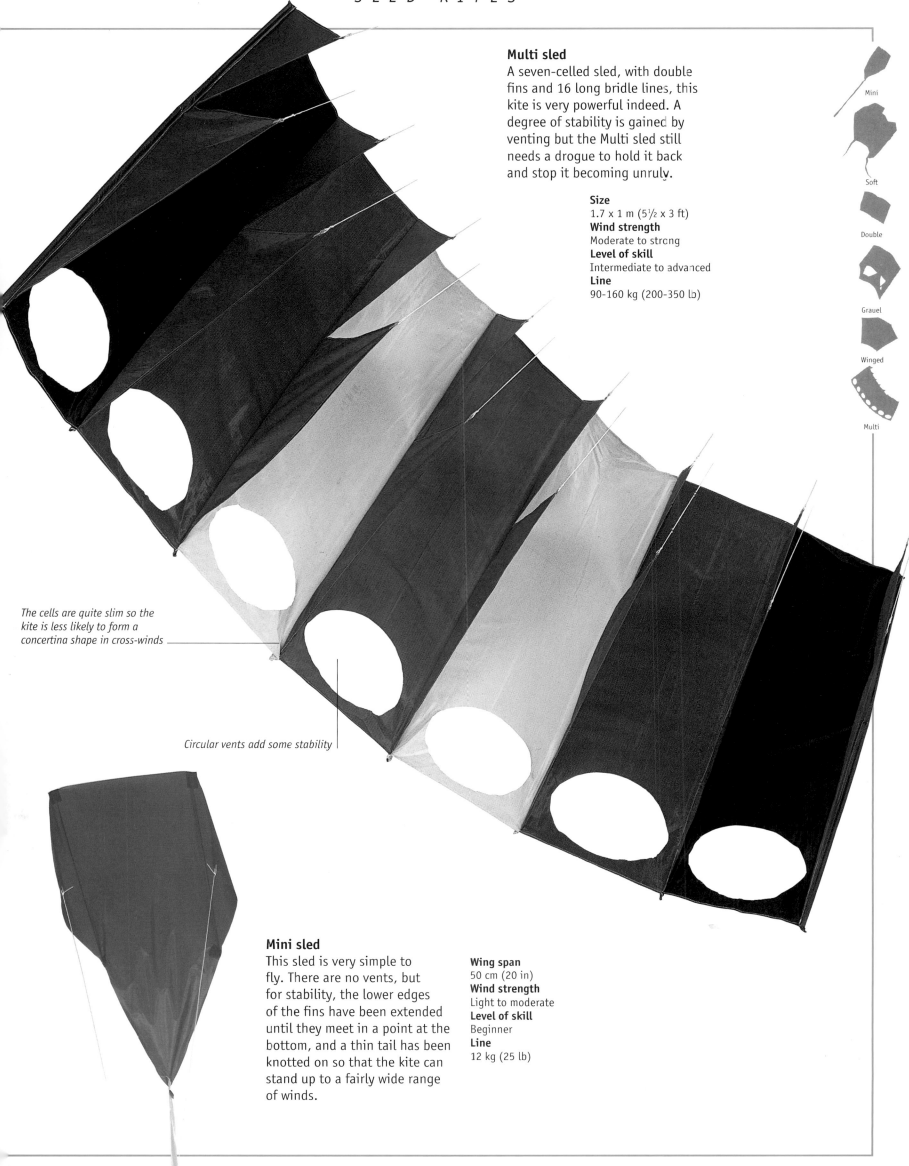

Multi sled
A seven-celled sled, with double fins and 16 long bridle lines, this kite is very powerful indeed. A degree of stability is gained by venting but the Multi sled still needs a drogue to hold it back and stop it becoming unruly.

Size
1.7 x 1 m (5½ x 3 ft)
Wind strength
Moderate to strong
Level of skill
Intermediate to advanced
Line
90-160 kg (200-350 lb)

Mini

Soft

Double

Grauel

Winged

Multi

The cells are quite slim so the kite is less likely to form a concertina shape in cross-winds

Circular vents add some stability

Mini sled
This sled is very simple to fly. There are no vents, but for stability, the lower edges of the fins have been extended until they meet in a point at the bottom, and a thin tail has been knotted on so that the kite can stand up to a fairly wide range of winds.

Wing span
50 cm (20 in)
Wind strength
Light to moderate
Level of skill
Beginner
Line
12 kg (25 lb)

DELTA KITES

With a large flexible wing area, the graceful delta is very efficient and will fly in the lightest of winds. Some deltas with very light spars will glide on thermals - rising currents of warm air - without any wind. As the thermal passes, the kite can be slowly wound in, giving enough windspeed to keep it in the air until another thermal is found. Other deltas stand up to a wide range of winds and can lift cameras.

Dan Leigh delta

A high-performance delta based on a hang-glider, the Dan Leigh flies well in even very light winds. The streamlined kite has a wide nose and an extended keel. Drag, or resistance, is not a problem as the cross-spar fits tightly, holding the cover taut.

Wing span
2 m (6½ ft)
Wind strength
Light
Level of skill
Intermediate
Line
27 kg (60 lb)

Leading edge

The trailing edge gently curves on either side in flight

A keel extends below the main body of the kite, adding stability

Fish delta

An attractively appliquéd fish kite with a keel for a fin. Where the leading edge spars finish, the cover is tapered to the nose. The tail is held open with light fibreglass rods, like the tail of a fighter.

Wing span
1.6 m (5¼ ft)
Wind strength
Light to moderate
Level of skill
Intermediate
Line
27 kg (60 lb)

Conyne delta

A variation on a standard triangular-shaped delta, the Conyne has a box section between two spars, which gives the kite extra stability.

Wing span
2.7 m (9 ft)
Wind strength
Light to moderate
Level of skill
Beginner to intermediate
Line
25 kg (50 lb)

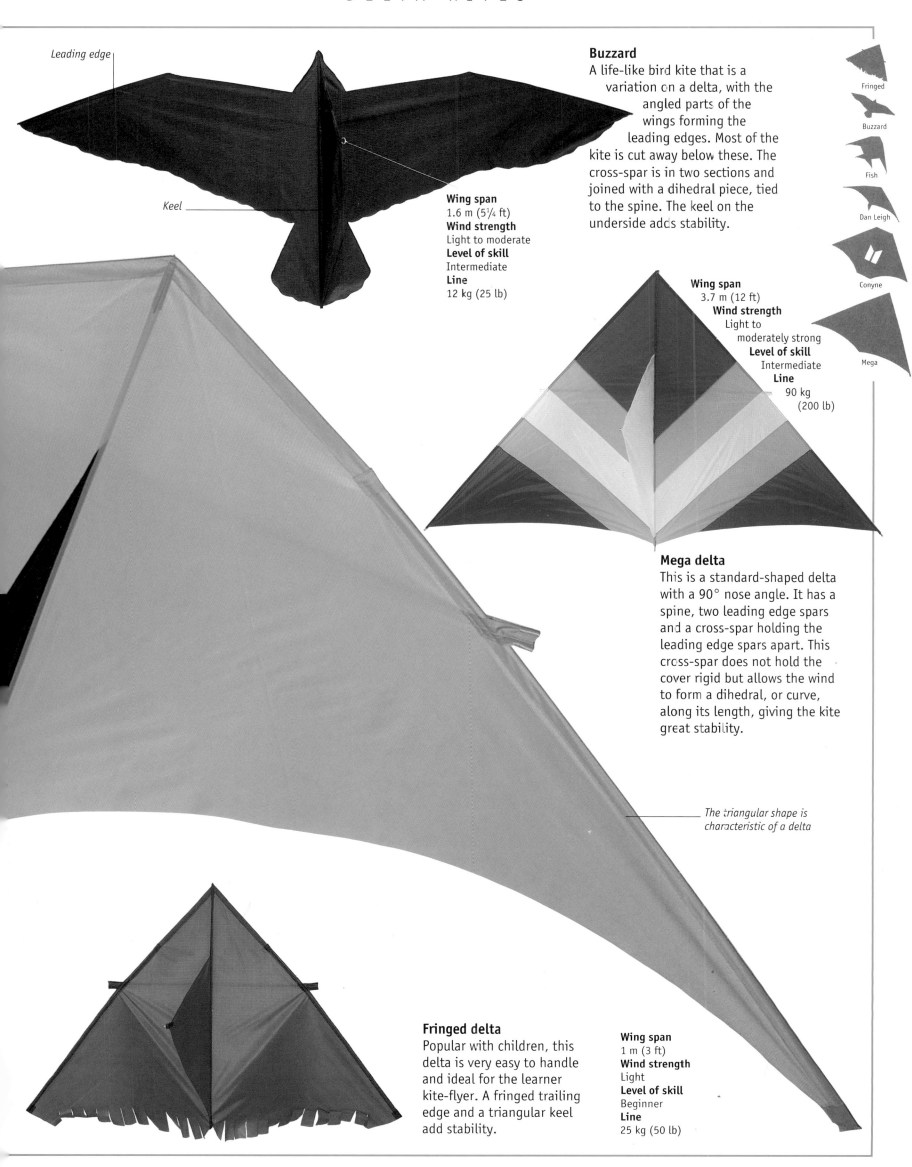

Leading edge

Keel

Wing span
1.6 m (5¼ ft)
Wind strength
Light to moderate
Level of skill
Intermediate
Line
12 kg (25 lb)

Buzzard

A life-like bird kite that is a variation on a delta, with the angled parts of the wings forming the leading edges. Most of the kite is cut away below these. The cross-spar is in two sections and joined with a dihedral piece, tied to the spine. The keel on the underside adds stability.

Fringed

Buzzard

Fish

Dan Leigh

Conyne

Mega

Wing span
3.7 m (12 ft)
Wind strength
Light to moderately strong
Level of skill
Intermediate
Line
90 kg (200 lb)

Mega delta

This is a standard-shaped delta with a 90° nose angle. It has a spine, two leading edge spars and a cross-spar holding the leading edge spars apart. This cross-spar does not hold the cover rigid but allows the wind to form a dihedral, or curve, along its length, giving the kite great stability.

The triangular shape is characteristic of a delta

Fringed delta

Popular with children, this delta is very easy to handle and ideal for the learner kite-flyer. A fringed trailing edge and a triangular keel add stability.

Wing span
1 m (3 ft)
Wind strength
Light
Level of skill
Beginner
Line
25 kg (50 lb)

SOFT KITES

Most soft kites are derived from the Parafoil kite, originally designed in the 1960s. This is radically different from other kites, as it has no frame to hold it rigid and is inflated by the wind. The Parafoil is basically an aerofoil: a cross-section of the kite is similar to the streamlined shape of an aeroplane wing, improving the kite's efficiency in the air. Soft kites are very powerful and have been used to lift cameras, radios, weather-forecasting equipment and even people.

Wing span
3.5 m (11 ft)
Wind strength
Moderate
Level of skill
Intermediate to
advanced
Line
90 kg (200 lb)

Snoopy stunter
Quite a complex kite composed of two Parafoils - one for each wing - and a large windsock down the centre. As a stunter it is not particularly efficient but as a spectacle in the sky it is second to none.

Slow but spectacular
A kite for display, and not performance stunting, the Snoopy stunter manoeuvres slowly in the sky.

Aerofoil
section

Keels sewn to the kite face held in shape by a system of bridles add stability

Tubular cell

Parafoil
The multi-cellular Parafoil comes in a wide range of sizes: the smallest can be held in the hand, the largest have to be held down by trucks. The number of cells and keels on each cell varies from kite to kite. The larger the kite, the greater the number of cells and keels.

Size
60 x 92 cm (24 x 36 in)
Wind strength
Moderate to strong
Level of skill
Beginner
Line
25 kg (50 lb)

Three long windsocks - wind-inflated tubes - give stability

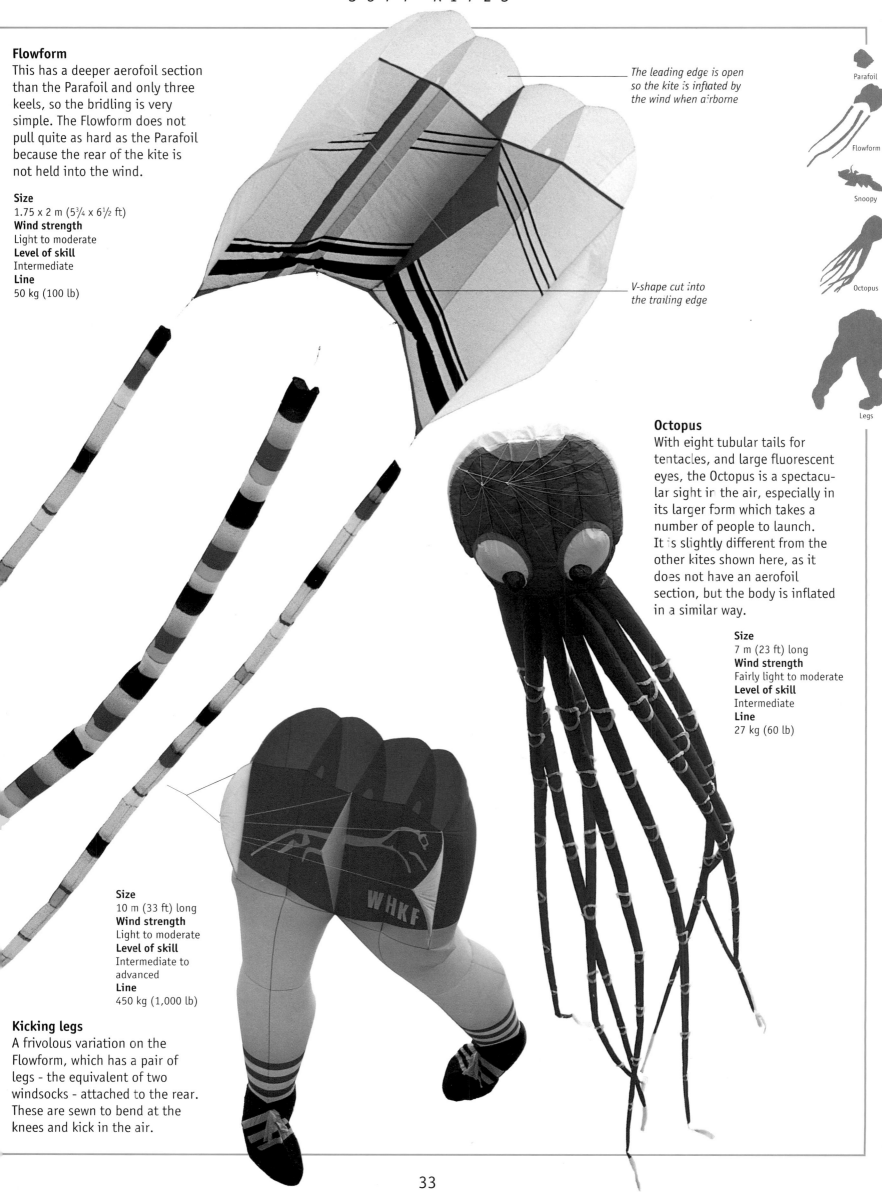

Flowform

This has a deeper aerofoil section than the Parafoil and only three keels, so the bridling is very simple. The Flowform does not pull quite as hard as the Parafoil because the rear of the kite is not held into the wind.

Size
1.75 x 2 m (5³/₄ x 6¹/₂ ft)
Wind strength
Light to moderate
Level of skill
Intermediate
Line
50 kg (100 lb)

The leading edge is open so the kite is inflated by the wind when airborne

V-shape cut into the trailing edge

Parafoil

Flowform

Snoopy

Octopus

Legs

Octopus

With eight tubular tails for tentacles, and large fluorescent eyes, the Octopus is a spectacular sight in the air, especially in its larger form which takes a number of people to launch. It is slightly different from the other kites shown here, as it does not have an aerofoil section, but the body is inflated in a similar way.

Size
7 m (23 ft) long
Wind strength
Fairly light to moderate
Level of skill
Intermediate
Line
27 kg (60 lb)

Size
10 m (33 ft) long
Wind strength
Light to moderate
Level of skill
Intermediate to advanced
Line
450 kg (1,000 lb)

Kicking legs

A frivolous variation on the Flowform, which has a pair of legs - the equivalent of two windsocks - attached to the rear. These are sewn to bend at the knees and kick in the air.

STUNT KITES

Ever since two-line steerable kites became available, more and more people have been attracted to this skilful and creative extension to kite-flying. The Peter Powell stunt kite is still a classic, while the introduction of delta-winged stunters has popularized stunt-flying as a competitive sport. Two-line stunters are steered by pulling to the left or right. Recently four-line stunters have become available, steered by adjusting the flight angle on either side of the kite so speed is controlled as well as direction. The structure of a kite determines its performance: some are designed for precise movement, others for speed. All are highly manoeuvrable, enabling them to perform spectacular displays of aerial acrobatics.

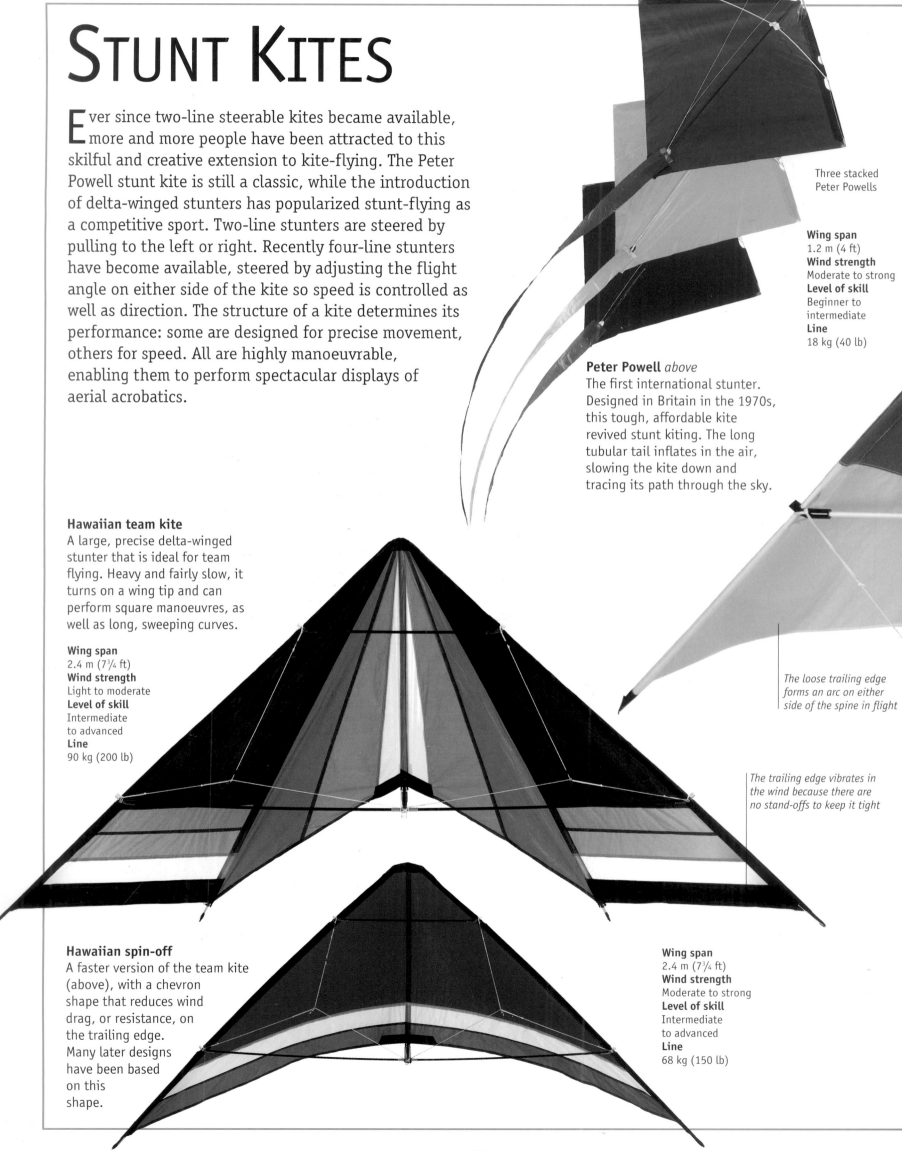

Three stacked
Peter Powells

Wing span
1.2 m (4 ft)
Wind strength
Moderate to strong
Level of skill
Beginner to
intermediate
Line
18 kg (40 lb)

Peter Powell *above*
The first international stunter.
Designed in Britain in the 1970s,
this tough, affordable kite
revived stunt kiting. The long
tubular tail inflates in the air,
slowing the kite down and
tracing its path through the sky.

Hawaiian team kite
A large, precise delta-winged
stunter that is ideal for team
flying. Heavy and fairly slow, it
turns on a wing tip and can
perform square manoeuvres, as
well as long, sweeping curves.

Wing span
2.4 m (7¾ ft)
Wind strength
Light to moderate
Level of skill
Intermediate
to advanced
Line
90 kg (200 lb)

*The loose trailing edge
forms an arc on either
side of the spine in flight*

*The trailing edge vibrates in
the wind because there are
no stand-offs to keep it tight*

Hawaiian spin-off
A faster version of the team kite
(above), with a chevron
shape that reduces wind
drag, or resistance, on
the trailing edge.
Many later designs
have been based
on this
shape.

Wing span
2.4 m (7¾ ft)
Wind strength
Moderate to strong
Level of skill
Intermediate
to advanced
Line
68 kg (150 lb)

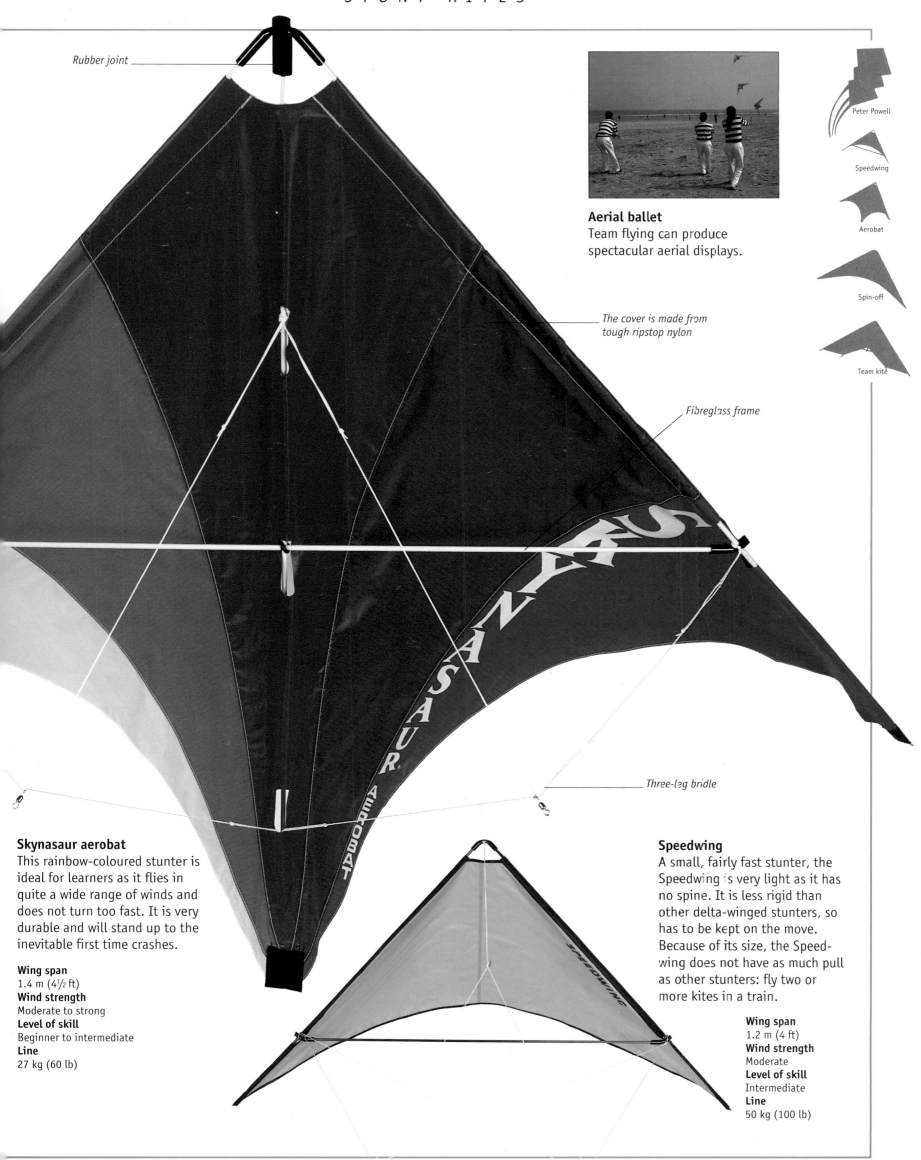

Rubber joint

Aerial ballet
Team flying can produce
spectacular aerial displays.

Peter Powell

Speedwing

Aerobat

Spin-off

Team kite

The cover is made from
tough ripstop nylon

Fibreglass frame

Three-leg bridle

Skynasaur aerobat
This rainbow-coloured stunter is
ideal for learners as it flies in
quite a wide range of winds and
does not turn too fast. It is very
durable and will stand up to the
inevitable first time crashes.

Wing span
1.4 m (4½ ft)
Wind strength
Moderate to strong
Level of skill
Beginner to intermediate
Line
27 kg (60 lb)

Speedwing
A small, fairly fast stunter, the
Speedwing is very light as it has
no spine. It is less rigid than
other delta-winged stunters, so
has to be kept on the move.
Because of its size, the Speedwing does not have as much pull
as other stunters: fly two or
more kites in a train.

Wing span
1.2 m (4 ft)
Wind strength
Moderate
Level of skill
Intermediate
Line
50 kg (100 lb)

STUNT KITES

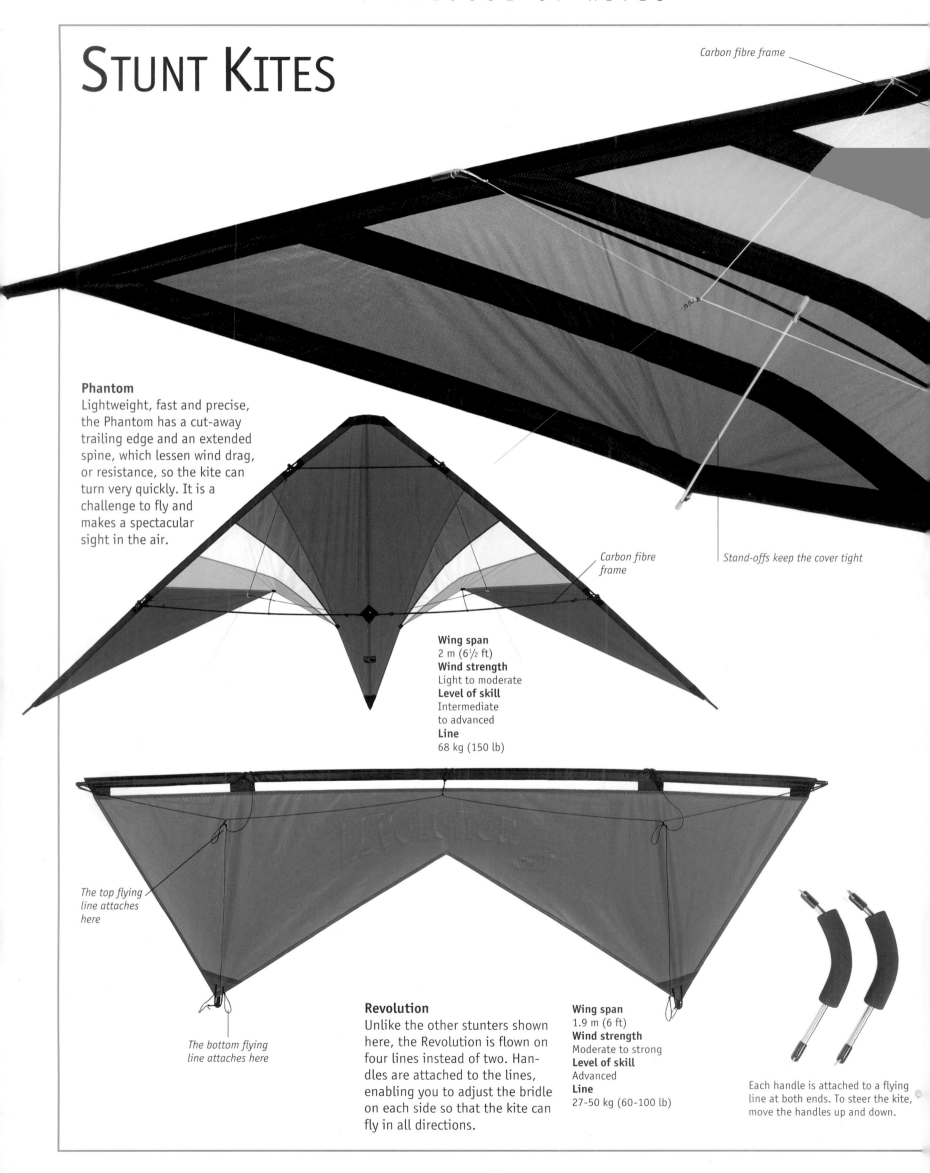

Carbon fibre frame

Phantom
Lightweight, fast and precise, the Phantom has a cut-away trailing edge and an extended spine, which lessen wind drag, or resistance, so the kite can turn very quickly. It is a challenge to fly and makes a spectacular sight in the air.

Carbon fibre frame

Stand-offs keep the cover tight

Wing span
2 m (6½ ft)
Wind strength
Light to moderate
Level of skill
Intermediate to advanced
Line
68 kg (150 lb)

The top flying line attaches here

The bottom flying line attaches here

Revolution
Unlike the other stunters shown here, the Revolution is flown on four lines instead of two. Handles are attached to the lines, enabling you to adjust the bridle on each side so that the kite can fly in all directions.

Wing span
1.9 m (6 ft)
Wind strength
Moderate to strong
Level of skill
Advanced
Line
27-50 kg (60-100 lb)

Each handle is attached to a flying line at both ends. To steer the kite, move the handles up and down.

Flexifoil

A unique design, the Flexifoil is a fast, exciting kite, which is extremely powerful when flown stacked in a colourful train. The kite has a single tapered cross-spar along the leading edge. Like the Parafoil (see page 32), it relies on the wind to give it shape in flight.

Paraflex

Revolution

Flexifoil

Phantom

Lite flite

Cross-spar

Cell

Four stacked Flexifoils

Size
1.2-3.7 m (4-12 ft) across
Wind strength
Light to moderate
Level of skill
Intermediate to advanced
Line
68 kg (150 lb)

Paraflex

With many cells that are inflated by the wind in flight, the Paraflex is basically a stunting Parafoil. It is a similar shape to the Flexifoil but does not have the cross-spar. As it is totally soft, it can be taken anywhere.

Size
1.9 m (6 ft) across
Wind strength
Moderate to strong
Level of skill
Intermediate to advanced
Line
36 kg (80 lb)

The V-shape cut into the trailing edge adds stability

Lite flite

A slow, precise stunter, the Lite Flite is one of the most modern kites available. It can turn on a wing tip, and was designed for team flying in very light winds.

Wing span
2.2 m (7 ft)
Wind strength
Light to moderate
Level of skill
Intermediate to advanced
Line
36-68 kg (80-150 lb)

PAPER & PLASTIC KITES

Everyday materials such as paper and plastic lend themselves perfectly to kite-making. Newspapers, wrapping paper, even refuse sacks can be used to create simple, though fragile, kites in any size. Involving little more than folding up paper or cutting a shape out of plastic, these kites are fun for children to make. Fly the kites in a light wind on sewing thread line.

Single-fold kite
The simplest paperfold kite, which is basically a rectangle of paper with a fold up the centre. A single-point bridle has been threaded on and a plastic tail attached to each bottom corner of the kite. The top edge is reinforced with tape.

The centre fold runs from the bottom to about two thirds of the way up

Tail made from strips of a plastic bag stuck together

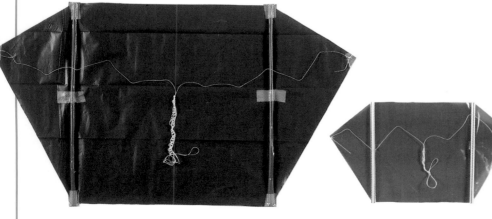

Plastic sled
Two varieties of the basic sled, one made from a green garden sack with rolled up plastic spars in a contrasting colour, the other cut from a carrier bag with drinking straw spars. The towing points are reinforced with tape.

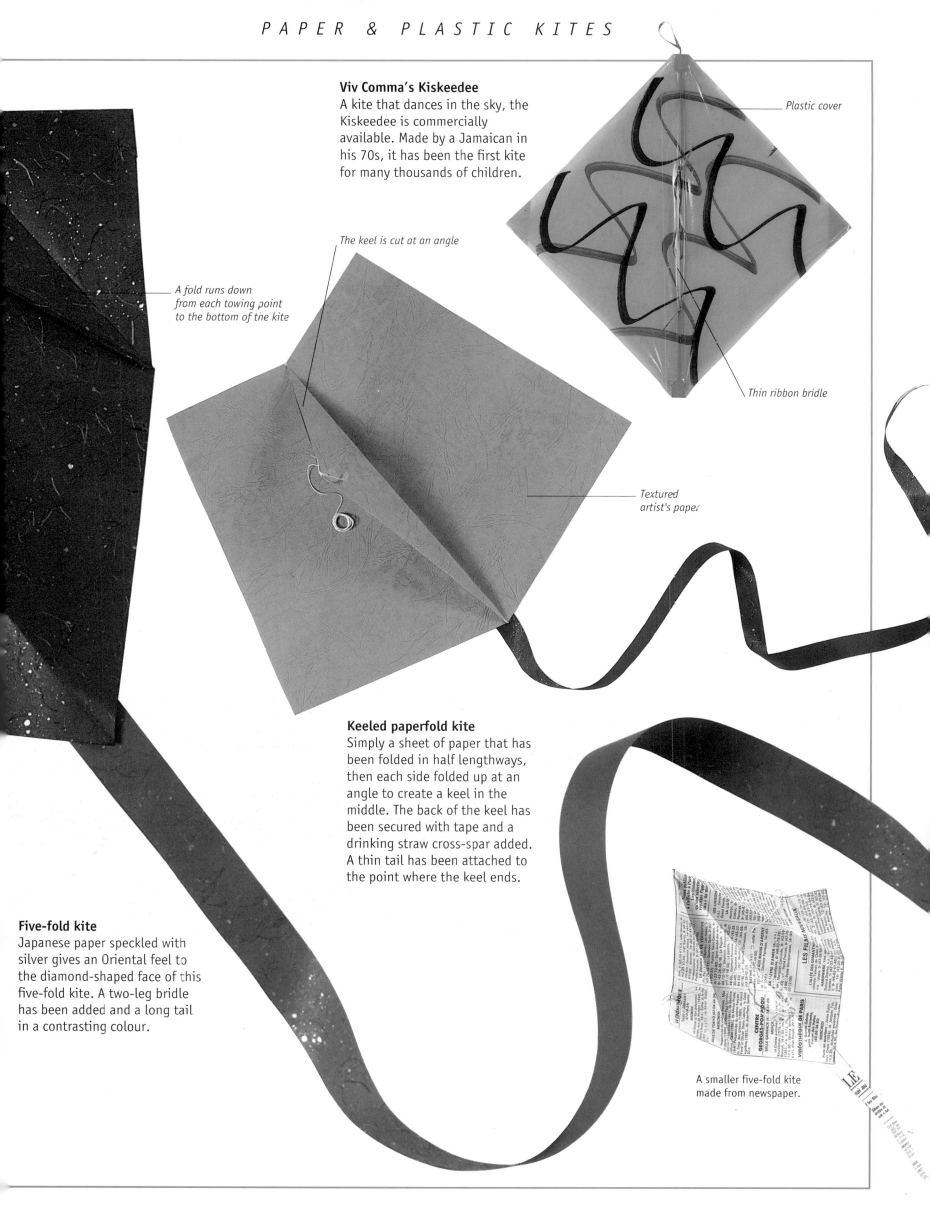

Viv Comma's Kiskeedee
A kite that dances in the sky, the Kiskeedee is commercially available. Made by a Jamaican in his 70s, it has been the first kite for many thousands of children.

Plastic cover

The keel is cut at an angle

A fold runs down from each towing point to the bottom of the kite

Thin ribbon bridle

Textured artist's paper

Keeled paperfold kite
Simply a sheet of paper that has been folded in half lengthways, then each side folded up at an angle to create a keel in the middle. The back of the keel has been secured with tape and a drinking straw cross-spar added. A thin tail has been attached to the point where the keel ends.

Five-fold kite
Japanese paper speckled with silver gives an Oriental feel to the diamond-shaped face of this five-fold kite. A two-leg bridle has been added and a long tail in a contrasting colour.

A smaller five-fold kite made from newspaper.

EQUIPMENT FOR FLYING

From basic handles, stunt straps and spools to some of the latest kite-flying gadgetry, such as night lights and wind-speed indicators, the choice of flying equipment is wide and at times confusing. These pages illustrate the options available, highlighting differences between similar pieces of equipment to enable you to choose the right accessories for your kite.

HANDLES

Flying line attaches here

Standard plastic handles
These lightweight handles are ideal for small kites as they may break under the strain of a larger kite being wound in.

Wooden handles
For large kites such as the Mega delta. Not for stunters.

Sky claws
A cross between a handle and a wrist strap (see above right), sky claws are good for small to medium stunters. For storage, they are slotted on to a bar, which is rotated to wind in the lines.

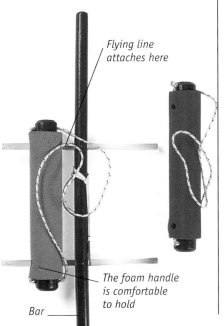

Flying line attaches here

Heavy-duty plastic handles
More comfortable and long-lasting than the standard variety, these handles are tailor-made for medium to large stunt kites.

Bar

The foam handle is comfortable to hold

STRAPS

Line is tied to the D-ring

Comfortable padded strap

Thin webbing strap

Wrist straps
An alternative to handles when stunting, wrist straps ease finger strain if flying for long periods. Thin straps are good for smaller stunters, padded straps for larger ones. Line cannot be stored on a strap: it has to be wound on to a spool or handle.

Wearing the strap
Slip the strap over your wrist and hold on to it below the D-ring.

Hole for index and middle fingers

Finger straps
Similar to wrist straps but worn on the fingers, these are more responsive to the feel of a stunt kite. They are only comfortable when flying in light winds.

SPOOLS & REELS

Three large holes in the centre help you grip more easily

Plastic spools
Available in different sizes, circular spools allow you to let out and wind in line quickly. Not suitable for large kites as the spool will not store enough line.

Using the spool
Hold the spool vertically in one hand. To let out line, point the wider rim of the spool towards the kite. To stop line, hold the spool vertically again.

Handle, for winding in line

Wooden deep-sky reel
A heavy reel with a rotating centre around which line is tied. Hold the reel in one hand, with your fingers stopping the centre from moving. To release line, let go of the centre.

TAILS, DROGUES & WINDSOCKS

FLYING ACCESSORIES

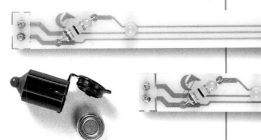

Night lights
To extend flying hours, battery-powered lights can be fitted on to a kite or line. They must be lightweight so that the kite's performance is not affected. Quite complex light systems are available.

Gloves
Gardening gloves are ideal to stop line burning your fingers.

Standard drogue

Drogues
Usually made of nylon, cone- or cup-shaped drogues add stability.

Sunglasses
Invest in a good quality pair; sometimes it is difficult to see the kite because of the brightness of the sky.

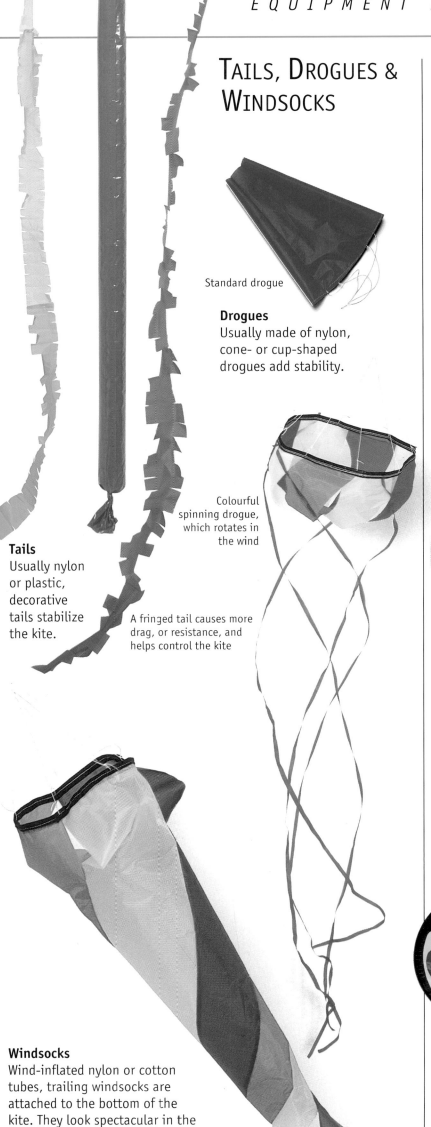

Colourful spinning drogue, which rotates in the wind

Line is tied to the triangle at the top

Dog spike
This spiral of metal screws into the ground and is useful for staking a single-line kite.

Wind-speed indicator
Basically a small propeller, held up to the wind to measure its speed at ground level.

Tails
Usually nylon or plastic, decorative tails stabilize the kite.

A fringed tail causes more drag, or resistance, and helps control the kite

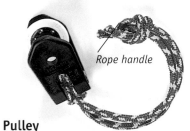

Rope handle

Parachuting teddy
This brave toy is attached to the line and then parachutes to earth. A crowd-puller.

Pulley
Clipped over the line, this is good for retrieving large single-line kites.

Windsocks
Wind-inflated nylon or cotton tubes, trailing windsocks are attached to the bottom of the kite. They look spectacular in the sky and add stability.

Messenger
A small butterfly-shaped sail, which is attached to the bottom of the line, and flies up to the top, releasing an object such as a glider. It then slides back.

FLYING KITES

This section shows you how to launch, control and land different types of kite, with tips for overcoming common problems and faults. It explains how to assess wind conditions and choose the best place to fly. It also includes an introduction to the exciting art of stunt-flying, with instructions for classic manoeuvres such as looping the loop and power diving.

HOW A KITE FLIES

A kite is heavier than air, so to fly, it needs lift, an upward force from the wind that is greater than the pull of gravity keeping it on the ground. For maximum lift, position the face at the correct angle to the wind (the angle of attack) by setting the ring accurately on the bridle. The best point for the ring is usually about a third of the way down the kite, but small adjustments can be made for varying winds. Even with the bridle pre-set, the angle of attack changes after launch, until the kite reaches its most efficient flying position.

THE ARC OF FLIGHT

In flight, the kite is affected by three main forces: lift, gravity, and drag. Lift is an upward force created by wind pressure on the face, which makes the kite rise and keeps it in the air. Gravity is the downward force on the kite, which works against lift. Drag is air resistance to the kite as it travels forwards. The sequence below shows how the angle of attack changes as the kite climbs because of the shifting relation-ship between forces.

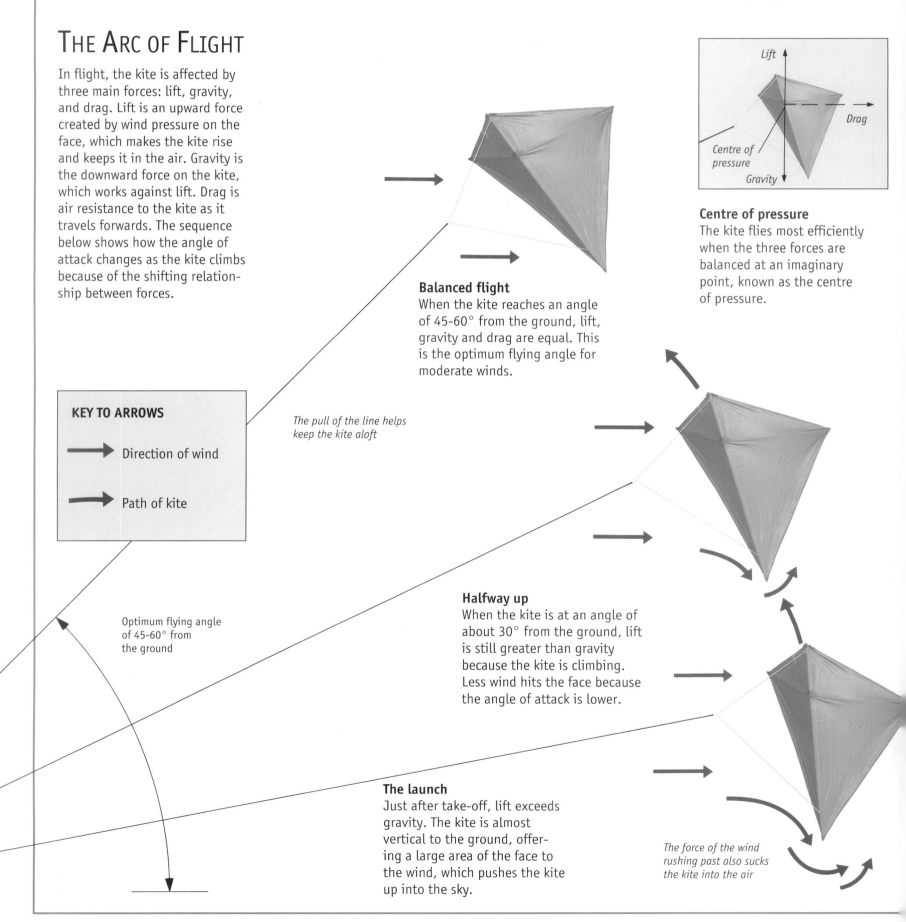

Centre of pressure
The kite flies most efficiently when the three forces are balanced at an imaginary point, known as the centre of pressure.

Lift

Drag

Centre of pressure

Gravity

Balanced flight
When the kite reaches an angle of 45-60° from the ground, lift, gravity and drag are equal. This is the optimum flying angle for moderate winds.

KEY TO ARROWS

→ Direction of wind

→ Path of kite

The pull of the line helps keep the kite aloft

Optimum flying angle of 45-60° from the ground

Halfway up
When the kite is at an angle of about 30° from the ground, lift is still greater than gravity because the kite is climbing. Less wind hits the face because the angle of attack is lower.

The launch
Just after take-off, lift exceeds gravity. The kite is almost vertical to the ground, offer-ing a large area of the face to the wind, which pushes the kite up into the sky.

The force of the wind rushing past also sucks the kite into the air

STAYING AIRBORNE

To remain aloft, a kite has to be kept pointing into the wind, so it requires directional stability. Some kites are inherently stable because of their design, others need stability added.

The widest part of the kite is at the bottom

Balloon keel, which is inflated by the wind to give stability

Triangular delta
The shape of the delta and its curved trailing edge help keep the kite flying almost horizontal to the ground - a low angle of attack.

The angled shape of the face adds stability

Classic diamond
To stay on a stable course, a diamond-shaped Malay kite has to be flown flat with a long tail or with an angled surface (a tail is then optional).

Two-celled box
A rigid box kite has many surfaces that give the kite lift and stability.

The back cell keeps the front cell facing into the wind

Flat kite
To stay in the air, a flat kite needs a tail.

SETTING THE BRIDLE

Position the bridle approximately first, then fine-tune it on the field.

Normal towing point

20-30°

Hold the kite by the ring

1 Lay the kite on its back. Put your finger underneath the bridle line and carefully move your hand up the line to lift the top of the kite.

2 When the top of the kite is at an angle of 20-30° from the ground, tie a ring to the place where your finger is with a lark's head knot (see page 65). The ring becomes the towing point. This is usually about a third of the way down the length of the kite and stands off from the face by about half the length.

3 Test the kite for flight by holding it into the wind. If the wind lifts the kite, the bridle is in the right position.

ADJUSTING THE TOWING POINT

The towing point may need to be adjusted to suit the wind conditions on site. However, only very slight adjustments are needed to change the angle of attack sufficiently: a maximum of 1 cm (½ in) from the normal towing point position.

Light winds
In light winds, move the ring down to expose more of the face to the wind.

Strong winds
If the wind is strong, move the ring towards the top of the kite. This will reduce wind pressure on the face.

PREPARING TO FLY

It is best to fly a kite on a flat, open site, which is free of obstructions, such as trees, buildings and overhead cables. If there are other flyers around - as there will be at festivals - choose the clearest part of the sky for launching the kite. Contrary to popular belief, you do not need a strong force of wind to make a kite fly: light to moderate breezes are best, although some kites, such as heavy boxes or more robust stunters, are designed for stronger winds. Always assess the wind speed before launching a kite.

CHOOSING A SITE

The ideal flying site is flat and without obstructions, for example a beach or moor in the countryside and a heath or large open park in a built-up area. Any trees or buildings in the wind's path will cause turbulence.

Flying by the sea
A beach is a great location for kite-flying with often nothing but the sand and sea for miles. Avoid cliffs because of turbulence.

The freedom of flying
Kite-flying in a wide open area gives a real sense of freedom.

KITE FLYER'S SAFETY CODE
▲ Choose an open site, never within three miles of an airfield.
▲ Do not fly near electric pylons or overhead cables.
▲ Do not fly in a thunderstorm: the kite could act as a lightning conductor.
▲ Avoid people and animals.
▲ Do not fly too near other kites unless stunting or kite-fighting.
▲ Wear protective gloves, especially for larger kites and in stronger winds as line can burn hands.
▲ Do not fly your kite over the legal limit in your country.

Open space
Although not completely free of obstructions, this city heath is a good flying site with any buildings well away from the flyer.

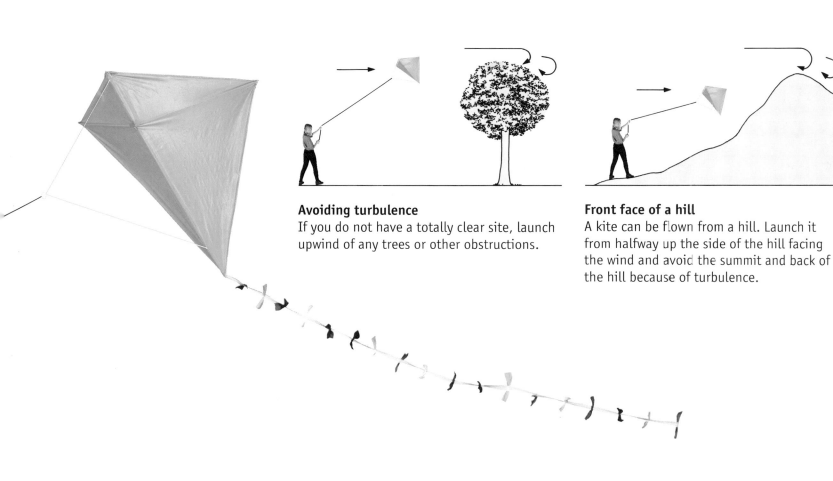

Avoiding turbulence
If you do not have a totally clear site, launch upwind of any trees or other obstructions.

Front face of a hill
A kite can be flown from a hill. Launch it from halfway up the side of the hill facing the wind and avoid the summit and back of the hill because of turbulence.

MEASURING WIND SPEED

As a general rule, most kites are designed to fly between certain windspeeds, although some will fly in a wide range of winds. To check the wind speed, either use a wind-speed indicator (see page 41) or the Beaufort Scale. This system, originally devised in 1805 by British Admiral Sir Francis Beaufort to record wind strength at sea, measures wind speed on land, using indicators such as trees and plumes of smoke. The scale starts from Force 0 (calm) and rises to Force 12 (hurricane). Do not fly a kite in winds stronger than Force 6 on the scale.

BEAUFORT WIND SCALE				
DESCRIPTION	VISUAL INDICATOR	SUITABLE KITES	WIND SPEED (m.p.h.)	FORCE
Calm	Smoke rises		under 1	0
Light air	Smoke drifts		2	1
Light breeze	Leaves rustle	A delta is good for light winds as it glides on the top of the wind.	5	2
Gentle breeze	Leaves move	Bowed kites are tailor-made for gentle to fresh winds.	10	3
Moderate breeze	Branches move		15	4
Fresh breeze	Small trees sway	Generally, box kites fly best in moderate to stronger winds.	21	5
Strong breeze	Large branches move		28	6

SINGLE-LINE KITES

Whether a box kite or a diamond-shaped Malay, single-line kites are easy to launch and retrieve. They make quite a spectacle in the sky, either let out on longer line or brought in closer to the ground. Before launching the kite, check that the bridle is set for flight (see page 45), the spars are seated securely in their pockets, the flying line is tied on properly and any tail is unravelled. Do not run with the kite to launch it, unless you want the exercise. If the kite starts to drop in the air, wind in line or step back and it will rise.

SHORT LAUNCHING

So-called because the kite is launched on a short length of line, this is the standard method for launching a single-line kite. If your kite does not lift, it is probably because it is too large, the wind is too light or there is ground turbulence, so try long launching.

LONG LAUNCHING

Launch a kite on a long length of line if short launching has failed or you are launching a large kite that is awkward to handle at close quarters. It is easiest to long launch with a helper.

Hold the kite in front of you

Hold the kite up and tilt it forwards slightly

Hold the kite at arm's length

Point the spool rim towards the kite so that line can slip off easily

Move the handle backwards and forwards to unwind line

Step back

1 Stand with your back to the wind, holding the kite in one hand and the handle or spool in the other.

2 Release the kite into the air, letting out a little line as you do so. The wind will catch the sail and lift the kite. Slowly pay out more line.

1 Hold the handle or spool, and ask your helper to take the kite and walk backwards downwind while you unravel 9-15 m (30-50 ft) of line.

2 When you give a signal, the helper should hold the kite up and gently release it. Move backwards or wind in line to help the kite climb.

STANDARD RETRIEVAL

This method can be used to retrieve a kite on a long or short flying line. With practice, the kite can be wound in so that it can be picked out of the sky, though in reality it may drop a little in front of you.

Wind in line

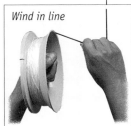

Spool faces kite

Let line run freely through your fingers

1 To retrieve the kite, simply wind in the flying line on to the handle or spool.

2 If turbulence causes the kite to dart around in the sky, let out line to stabilize the kite, then wind it in again.

WALKING THE KITE DOWN

If you try to bring the kite in using the standard method and find that there is too much pull, follow this procedure.

Tie the line securely to the stake

1 Anchor the flying line by tying it to a stake such as a dog spike or a tree.

3 When you reach the kite, put it on its back so that the wind will not lift it, unclip the pulley, and untie the flying line. Dismantle the kite.

2 Clip a pulley over the line, hold on to the handle below the pulley and walk downwind towards the kite. It will be pulled from the sky.

4 Go back to the anchor point and wind the flying line on to the handle or spool.

FIGHTER KITES

The competitive sport of kite-fighting goes back hundreds of years. Exciting and fun, it requires skill, quick responses and total concentration, otherwise the line of your kite will be cut by an opponent. If you are a beginner, tape a long plastic tail to the rear of your kite. This will slow down its reactions. As you become more skilled, shorten the tail. Eventually you will be able to do without one. Traditionally, fighters are flown on glass-coated line, but it is safer to use standard line for practice.

LAUNCHING A FIGHTER

It is easiest to launch a fighter with the help of a friend. Always have the wind behind you.

Kite climbs

Use one hand to release the kite

Hold the kite in front of you

Pull in line

Point the spool rim towards the kite

Point the spool rim towards the ground

Pile of line

1 Hold the handle or spool and ask your helper to take the kite and walk backwards downwind, while you unravel 9-15 m (30-50 ft) of line.

2 Let out some more line so that you have a pile at your feet. Put the handle or spool on the ground, slightly to one side of you.

3 Hold the line above the pile. When you give a signal, your helper should hold the kite up and gently let go.

4 Pull in the line hand over hand so that the kite climbs and clears ground turbulence.

MANOEUVRING A FIGHTER

The closer the kite is to you, the faster your reactions will have to be, so aim to get the kite to climb to 60 m (200 ft). You will probably have to repeat the following steps several times to do this. Once the kite reaches this height, practise controlling your fighter until you can make it go where you want it to.

TIPS FOR MANOEUVRING
▲ If the kite is flown far out to one side, it loses stability. Pull in line hand over hand and let it drop in the pile.
▲ Always have enough line in the pile to release suddenly if the kite dives to the ground from a low level.

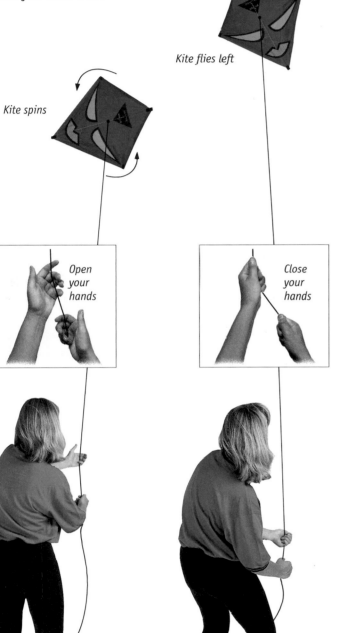

Kite flies left

Kite spins

Open your hands

Close your hands

1 Let line run freely through your fingers. The kite will spin and slowly lose height. It will travel downwind, releasing more line.

2 When the kite nose is pointing in the direction you want it to fly (up to gain height), stop the line. The kite will travel in that direction.

RETRIEVING A FIGHTER

Simply pull in line hand over hand and let it drop in the pile at your feet.

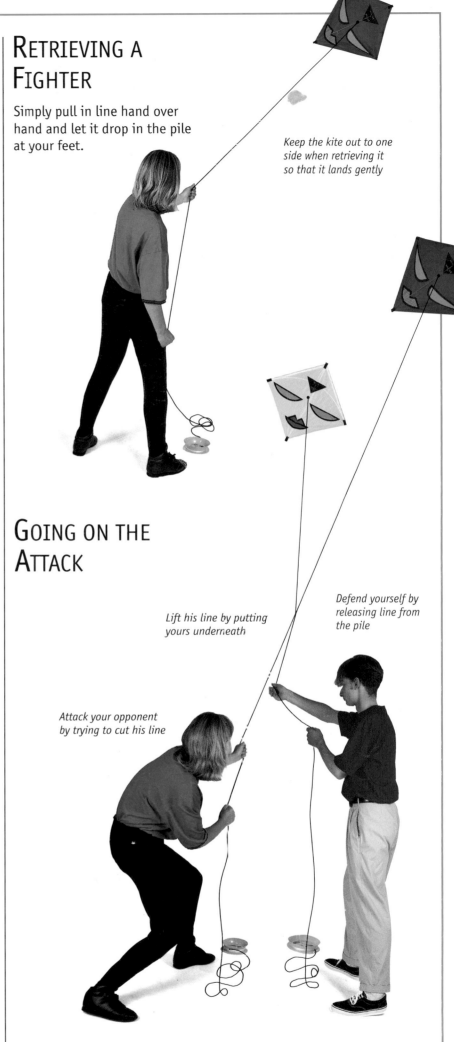

Keep the kite out to one side when retrieving it so that it lands gently

GOING ON THE ATTACK

Lift his line by putting yours underneath

Defend yourself by releasing line from the pile

Attack your opponent by trying to cut his line

The aim is to cut your opponent's line before he cuts yours. To do this, move your line very quickly over his. You will be at an advantage if you can lift his line by positioning yours underneath. If he attacks you, release line from your pile so that friction from his cut is spread over more of your line.

STUNT KITES

Controlling a stunt kite in even a basic manoeuvre adds another dimension to kite-flying. Once a single-line kite is launched, you can enjoy the spectacle, whereas a stunter needs constant steering to stay in the sky. As a rule, the kite lines should be 45-60 m (150-200 ft) long, although you may want to shorten them as you become more experienced; the shorter the lines, the quicker your reactions will have to be. If this is your first attempt at flying a stunter, get the feel of the kite before trying any manoeuvres.

SELF-LAUNCHING

Launching a stunt kite on your own is fairly simple. Always have the wind behind you, and also make sure that when the kite is laid out, the flying lines are exactly equal and not crossed.

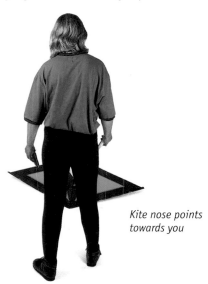

Kite nose points towards you

1 Put the kite face-down on the ground, and walk backwards upwind unravelling all the line off the handles.

2 Push a stake such as a dog spike or a tent peg into the ground and place the handles over it to hold them.

3 Return to the kite. Position it on the points on its base and lean it back slightly so that it is not lifted by the wind.

Choose a different coloured handle for each hand

Step back

4 Go back to the handles. Pick up the left handle in your left hand and the right handle in your right hand. Move back and the kite will take off.

TIPS FOR LAUNCHING
▲ During take-off, keep your hands together to steer the kite straight up.
▲ If the kite veers to either side, steer it back by pulling on the opposite line.
▲ The helper may prefer to rest the kite against his legs instead of holding it up.

LAUNCHING WITH A HELPER

Sometimes it is easiest to enlist the help of a friend when launching a stunter. Diamond-shaped stunt kites, such as the classic Peter Powell, have to be launched this way.

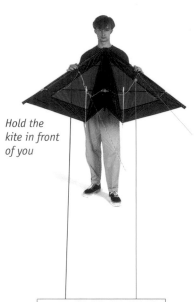

Hold the kite in front of you

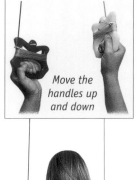

Move the handles up and down

1 Hold the handles and ask your helper to take the kite and walk backwards downwind while you unravel all the line off the handles.

STEERING

If this is your first launch, let the kite travel as high as it will go (if you practise a manoeuvre too close to the ground, you may crash the kite). Then, practise these basic steering movements to get the feel of the kite. Remember that when you steer, the direction the kite flies in will depend on its position in the sky. If you pull with your right hand, the kite will not necessarily go to the right side of the sky.

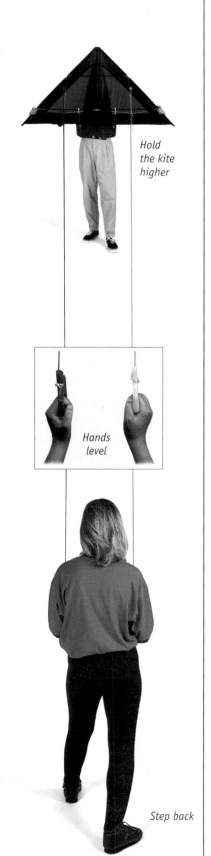

Hold the kite higher

Hands level

Step back

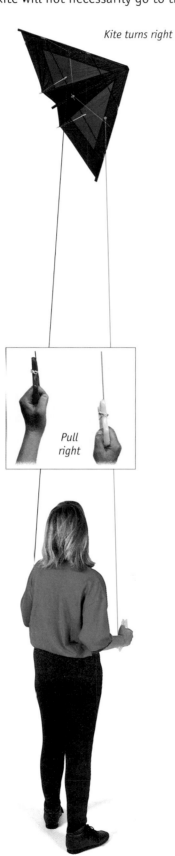

Kite turns right

Pull right

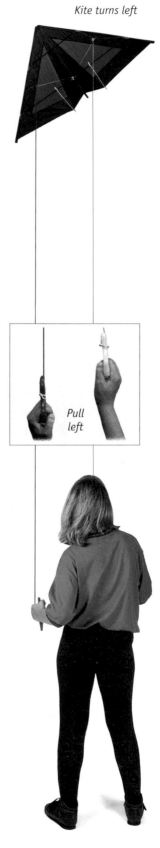

Kite turns left

Pull left

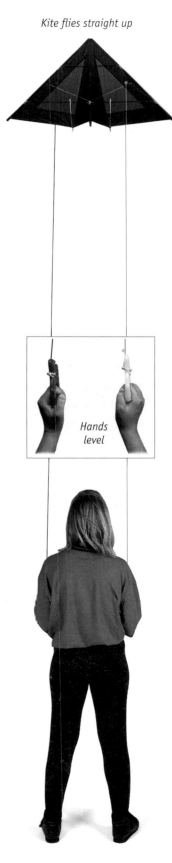

Kite flies straight up

Hands level

2 When you give a signal, the helper should hold the kite up and gently release it. Step back to pull it away from him.

Turning right
Pull gently with your right hand. The kite will steer right relative to its starting position.

Turning left
Pull gently with your left hand. The kite will steer left relative to its starting position.

Keeping on a straight course
Hold both hands together to go straight in any direction.

SIMPLE LOOP

The most basic stunt manoeuvre, the loop helps you to learn control of the kite. At first keep your hands close together so that the loop is quite large. Then try a smaller loop by keeping your hands further apart. When tracing a series of loops in one direction, do the same number in the opposite direction to unwrap the lines.

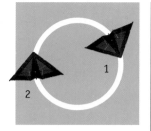

Loop manoeuvre

INFINITY

This simple figure of eight logically follows on from the basic loop. Trace the shape in the sky again and again to perfect your technique, aiming to keep the cross-over point directly downwind of you each time.

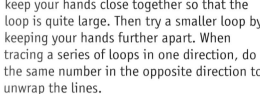

Nose points up

Kite looping

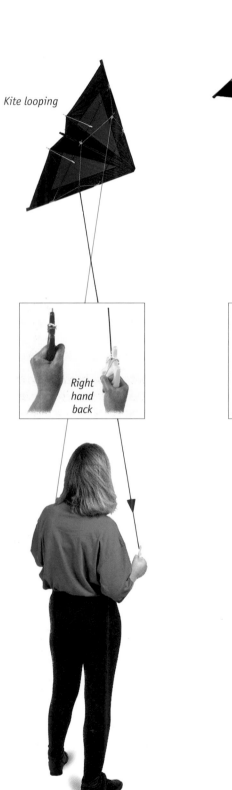

Right hand back

Hands level

Kite flies straight

Kite turns right

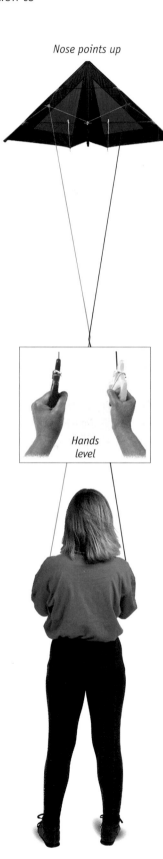

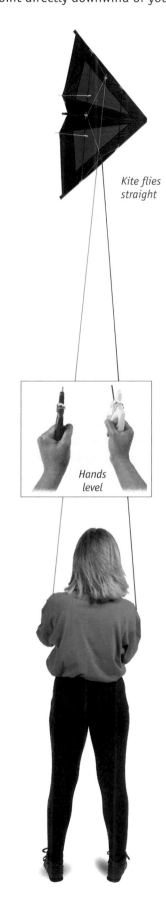

Hands level

Right hand back

1 Gently move your right hand back and keep it in this position so that the kite does a loop.

2 When the nose of the kite points up, bring your hands level. Let the kite travel to the highest point it can reach.

1 Start by holding both hands level so that the kite flies in a straight line.

2 Gently move your right hand back so that the kite turns to the right.

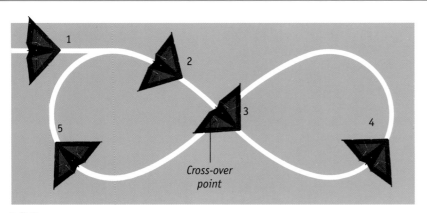

Infinity manoeuvre

HELPFUL TIPS FOR INFINITY

▲ Make sure your hands are the same distance apart so that both sides of the shape are the same size.

▲ Keep all hand movements gentle for good rounded curves.

▲ Vary the size of the figure by changing your hand distance.

BASIC LANDING

The easiest way to land a stunt kite safely, this simple method is invaluable for the learner stunt-flyer.

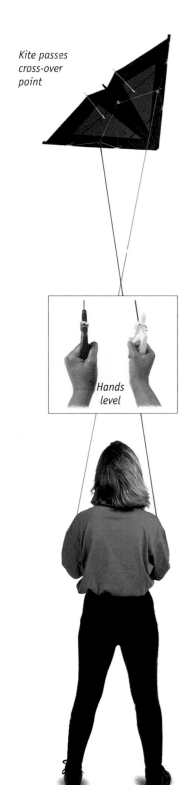

Kite passes cross-over point

Hands level

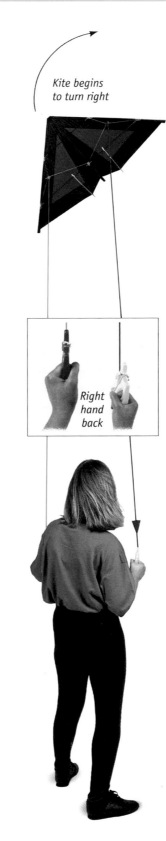

Kite begins to turn left

Left hand back

Kite begins to turn right

Right hand back

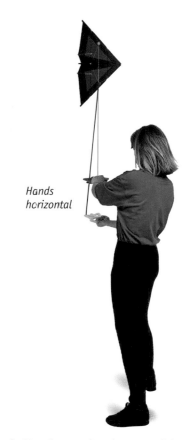

Hands horizontal

1 Keeping one hand on top of the other, steer the kite parallel to the ground as far as it will go.

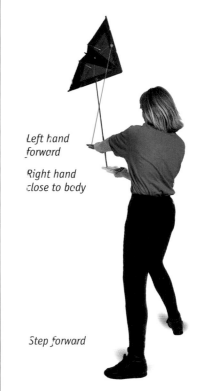

Left hand forward

Right hand close to body

Step forward

3 Move your right hand forward so that it is level with the left again. The kite will pass through the cross-over point.

4 Move your left hand back so the kite turns left. Then bring your hands level; the kite will pass the cross-over point again.

5 Gently move your right hand back and complete the right hand turn, returning to step 2.

2 When the kite reaches this point, bring your left hand forward and step forward. The kite will gently drop from the sky.

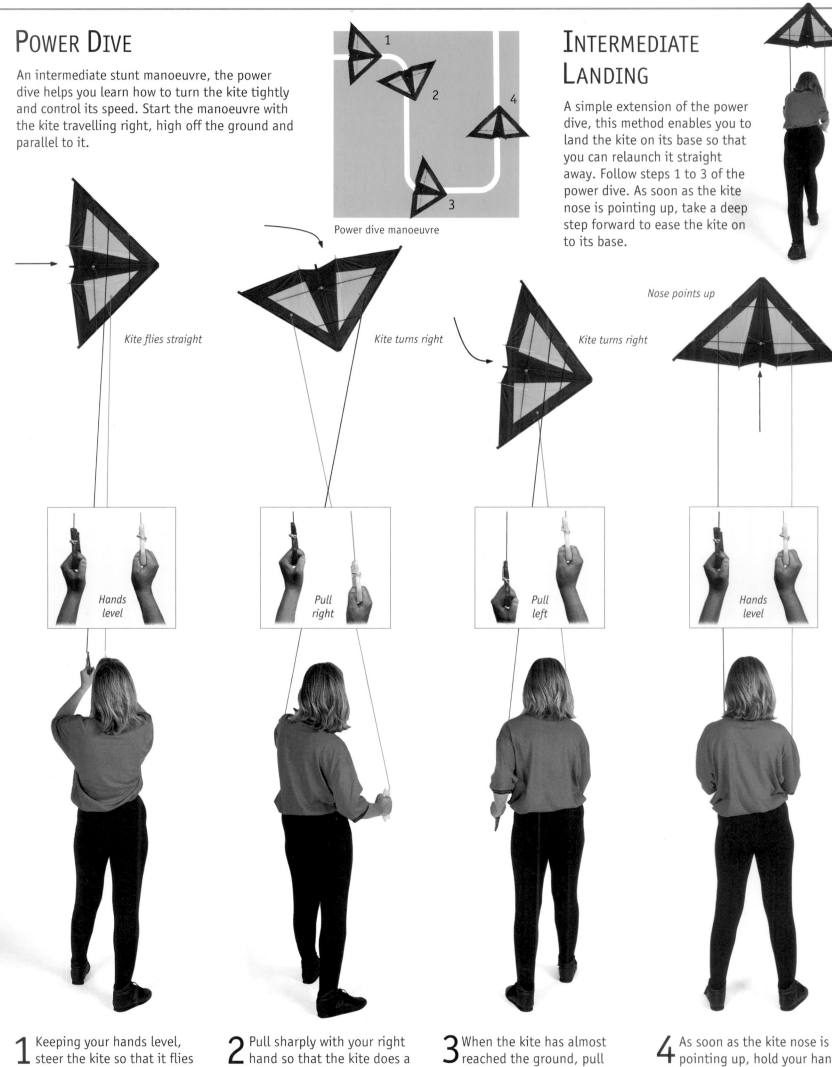

POWER DIVE

An intermediate stunt manoeuvre, the power dive helps you learn how to turn the kite tightly and control its speed. Start the manoeuvre with the kite travelling right, high off the ground and parallel to it.

Power dive manoeuvre

INTERMEDIATE LANDING

A simple extension of the power dive, this method enables you to land the kite on its base so that you can relaunch it straight away. Follow steps 1 to 3 of the power dive. As soon as the kite nose is pointing up, take a deep step forward to ease the kite on to its base.

Kite flies straight

Kite turns right

Kite turns right

Nose points up

Hands level

Pull right

Pull left

Hands level

1 Keeping your hands level, steer the kite so that it flies parallel to the ground.

2 Pull sharply with your right hand so that the kite does a tight right turn. Then bring your hands level. The kite will fly towards the ground.

3 When the kite has almost reached the ground, pull sharply with your left hand. The kite will turn to your right.

4 As soon as the kite nose is pointing up, hold your hands level. The kite will start to rise. Once it reaches the top of the line, the manoeuvre is complete.

SQUARE

To practise the power dive in another manoeuvre, try the square. Start this in the same way as the power dive. Aim for crisp 90° turns and keep the sides of the square straight by holding your hands at the same distance apart. The kite speed should be consistent throughout.

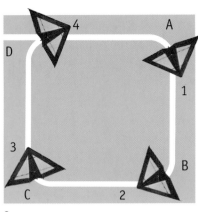

Square manoeuvre

TIPS FOR THE MANOEUVRES
▲ Initially, do not bring the kite too close to the ground as you may crash it.
▲ The kite's speed increases as it nears the ground. Move forwards to slow it down.
▲ The kite rises slowly as you have reversed the direction it is travelling in. Move back to increase its speed.

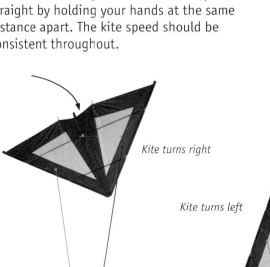

Kite turns right

Kite turns left

Kite begins to turn right

Kite turns right

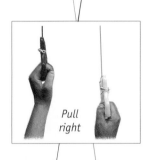

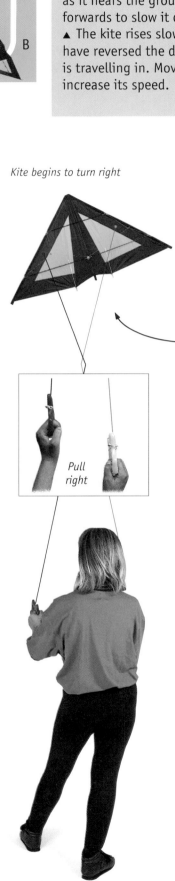

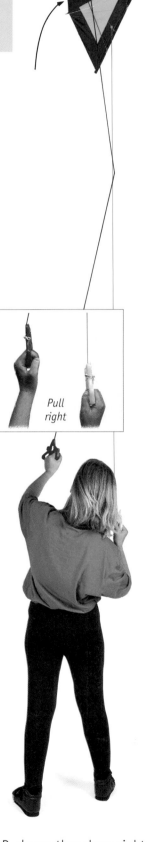

Pull right

1 Steer the kite parallel to the ground. At A, pull sharply with your right hand so the kite does a tight right turn. Bring your hands level so the kite flies straight.

2 At B, pull sharply with your right hand so that the kite turns to your left. Bring your hands level. The kite will fly parallel to the ground.

3 When the kite reaches C, pull right again to make the third corner of the square. Bring your hands level. The kite will rise.

4 At D, do another sharp right turn. Bring your hands level so that the kite flies straight and parallel to the ground again.

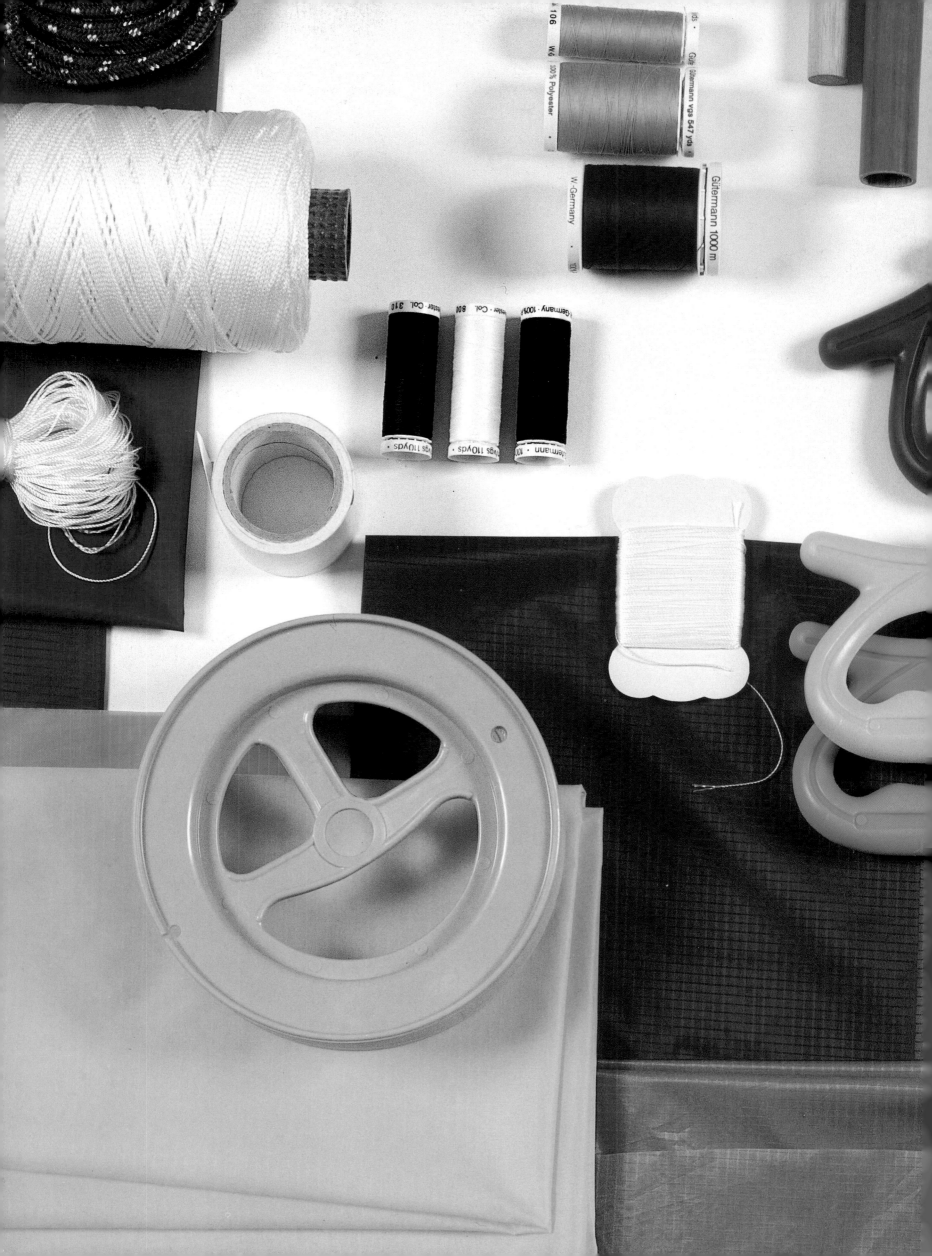

MAKING A KITE

Featuring patterns for five different kites, this section shows you step-by-step how to create your own kites. If this is your first attempt at kite-making, start with the sled or Della Porta, then progress on to one of the more complex designs. Choices for materials and equipment are highlighted in a visual glossary. A practical guide to basic techniques ensures a professional finish.

MATERIALS & EQUIPMENT

Most of the materials on these pages are available from specialist kite stores and mail order companies, although mountaineering shops can be a good source of tapes and thick climbing rope. The choice of materials depends on the type of kite you are making. Fibreglass rod, for example, is ideal for the flexible bow of a fighter, although inappropriate for the rigid frame of a box kite, where dowel is best. Kite-making equipment can generally be found around the home; some tools, such as a circle-cutter, give quick, accurate results but are not essential.

TAPES

Ripstop tape
Sticky-backed nylon. Useful for repairs, decoration or reinforcing weak points.

FABRICS & THREADS

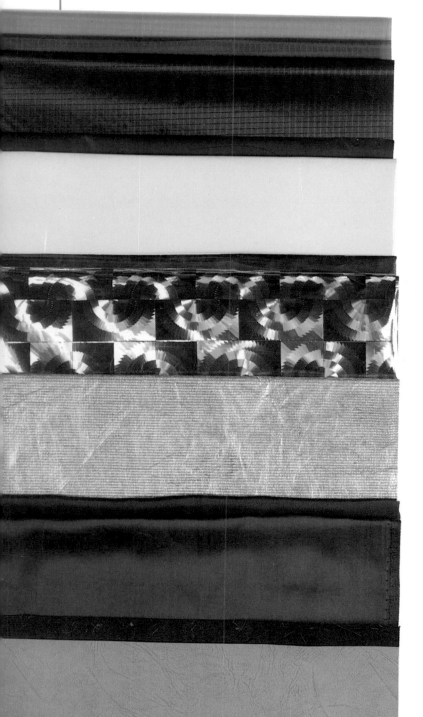

Ripstop nylon
Lightweight and strong, ripstop is the ideal covering material. It comes in a rainbow of colours.

Plastic
From carrier bags to heavy duty bin liners, plastic is a good, cheap covering material for simpler kites.

Mylar
A strong, light, manmade film that has less stretch than plastic. Ideal for simpler kites.

Tyvek
A synthetic material made in the same way as paper, Tyvek does not tear. Not widely available.

Silk
Used to make graceful kites since earliest times. Lightweight and exclusive but expensive and difficult to work.

Paper
From fine tissue to ornate origami papers, paper makes decorative but fragile kites.

Thread
Choose polyester thread as cotton will rot.

Reinforced tape
A tape with fibreglass strands, which is used to hold spars in place on simple kites and to secure plastic tubing on stunters.

Webbing
Reinforces the noses of stunters. Will also strengthen any other part of a large kite that takes a lot of wear and tear.

Dacron
Sewn on larger stunters to make sleeves for the leading edge spars. Will stand more abrasion than ripstop nylon.

Double-sided tape
Useful for repairs and reinforcement.

Sticky tape
Invaluable for making simple kites, where it is used to stick down spars and strengthen towing points.

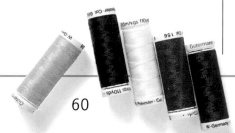

LINE

Nylon/polyester line
Cheap and widely available, this is the standard line. It comes smooth or coarse and in a variety of thicknesses and braids.

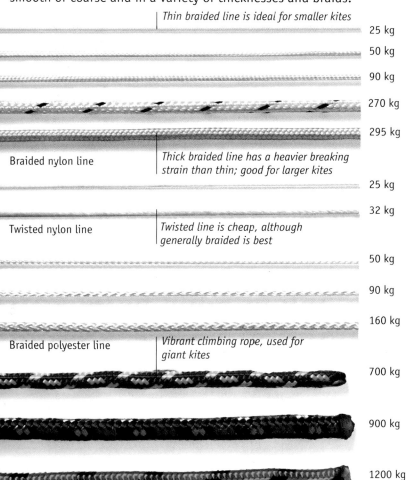

Thin braided line is ideal for smaller kites

	25 kg
	50 kg
	90 kg
	270 kg
	295 kg

Braided nylon line — *Thick braided line has a heavier breaking strain than thin; good for larger kites*

	25 kg
	32 kg

Twisted nylon line — *Twisted line is cheap, although generally braided is best*

	50 kg
	90 kg
	160 kg

Braided polyester line — *Vibrant climbing rope, used for giant kites*

	700 kg
	900 kg
	1200 kg

Climbing rope — *Twisted core surrounded by a braided sleeve*

Spectra
Braided from about 1,000 very fine polythene strands, spectra is much thinner and has less stretch than nylon/polyester line. Ideal for performance stunt-flying, where a quick response is essential. Spectra has to be protected with sleeving.

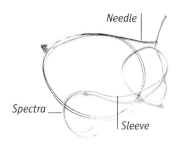

Green and pink spectra are colourful but coarser than white.

Smooth white spectra causes less friction when lines cross during stunting.

Sleeving
Nylon/polyester line from which the core has been removed, sleeving prevents spectra from cutting itself. Spectra is threaded through the sleeve with a special needle.

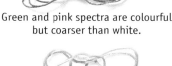

Needle

Spectra ⌐ Sleeve

Natural line
Not as durable as manmade line and heavier for the same breaking strain.

Glass-coated natural line adds a sharp cutting edge to fighters.

FRAMES & STRUCTURES

Fibreglass
Available as rod or tube. The rod is good for kites that need flex, such as fighters. The tube comes in two varieties: thin wall and thick wall.

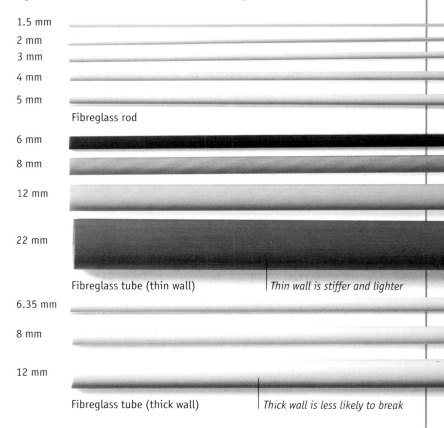

1.5 mm	
2 mm	
3 mm	
4 mm	
5 mm	

Fibreglass rod

6 mm	
8 mm	
12 mm	
22 mm	

Fibreglass tube (thin wall) — *Thin wall is stiffer and lighter*

6.35 mm	
8 mm	
12 mm	

Fibreglass tube (thick wall) — *Thick wall is less likely to break*

Carbon fibre
Stiff and light, carbon fibre is used on many of the latest high-tech stunters as it lasts well under stress.

5.5 mm	
8 mm	

Dowel
One of the best frame materials, dowel is easy to obtain, light and affordable. Choose ramin dowel or other hardwood varieties.

3 mm	
4 mm	
6 mm	
8 mm	
12 mm	
15 mm	

Bamboo
Like silk, a traditional material. The very thick stems are split down to size.

Piece of split bamboo

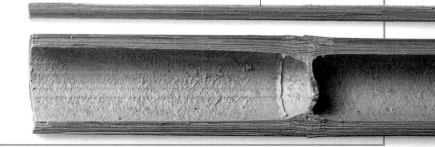

RINGS & SWIVELS

O rings

D rings

Split rings

Aluminium rings

An O ring is tied to the bridle and the line attached. A D ring is sewn in with a tab. Split rings are used on some box kites.

This part clips on to a ring on the kite

The line is tied on to the bottom loop

Standard swivels, for small to medium-sized kites and drogues.

Deep sea fishing swivel, good for large kites and spinning drogues.

Large fishing swivel

Swivel clips

An easy way to attach the flying line or a drogue to the kite. The clips rotate so line does not twist when wound in.

JOINTS

Ferruling

Tubing for joining spars in a straight line. Usually made from aluminium and cut to size.

The cross-spar slots in at each end

Dihedral pieces

V-shaped pieces keep the kite face at a constant angle.

Plastic tubing

Cut to an angle, this is used to join cross-spars to leading edge spars on stunters (see page 65).

OTHER ACCESSORIES

Sliders

Aluminium sliders help bow the cross-spar. The slider is threaded on to the line attached to the spar, and moved along the line to bow the spar.

Fluorescent beads are for night-flying

Beads

Strung on line attached to a tab on the cover, these tiny plastic beads are used to adjust tension on box kites. They slot behind the notch on a spar; the more beads behind the notch, the greater the tension.

End caps

Made from rubber, these are put on the ends of some spars to stop their abrasive edges rubbing against pockets and wearing through them.

Notches

These can be slotted on to the ends of a manmade spar, enabling it to house line.

62

EQUIPMENT

MARKING & MEASURING

Tailor's chalk
For marking out the cutting pattern on the fabric.

Felt-tip pen
An alternative to tailor's chalk. Choose a pen with a fine tip.

Card template for a sled

Template
Usually a plate or a cut-out shape from card, a template saves time when making more than one simple kite or cutting vents in the cover.

Ruler/set square
For transcribing the cutting pattern on to the fabric. It is important to be precise.

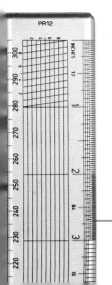

CUTTING

Scissors
Use sharp scissors for cutting fabric. Keep a pair specially for this purpose.

Circle cutter
Similar to a pair of compasses with a blade instead of a pencil, a circle cutter makes neat vents in ripstop nylon or plastic.

Soldering iron
Cutting nylon with a soldering iron seals the edges and stops them fraying. For speed, choose one with a rating of 30-40 W. A soldering iron can also be used for heat-sealing line.

Rotary cutter
A knife with a very fine rotating round blade for cutting ripstop nylon. Best used with a template.

Modelling knife
Used mainly to cut plastic, mylar and paper, as it can pull nylon.

OTHER EQUIPMENT

Hacksaw
Use a small hacksaw for cutting lengths of dowel and notches in the ends.

File
A small wood file is best for rounding the ends of dowel.

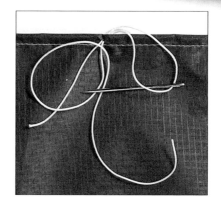

Lighter or matches
For heat-sealing the ends of line.

Wide-eyed needle
For threading line through tabs and the cover.

TECHNIQUES
See pages 64-5

Cutting

Heat-sealing

Preparing dowel

USEFUL TECHNIQUES

The practical techniques on these pages are essential for kite-making, enabling you to achieve truly professional results. Detailed steps demonstrate simple but effective methods for attaching spars to the cover, tying on a bridle, preparing dowel, heat-sealing line and cutting fabric. Pockets, tabs and reinforcing patches are easily made from scrap nylon; for speed, sew more than one tab or patch at a time. On larger kites, the fabric around the pocket or tab may need strengthening with extra layers of nylon.

MAKING A POCKET

A small fabric envelope, sewn to the cover at an angle, a pocket holds the end of a spar.

Nylon strip

Folded strip

1 Cut a strip of ripstop nylon, 18 cm (7 in) long and 2.5 cm (1 in) wide. Fold the strip over so that it is half its original length and repeat.

2 Pin the folded strip at a 45° angle to the kite edge, overlapping it by nearly half the length of the strip. Sew the strip to the kite across the corner of the kite.

The pocket should slightly overhang the kite edge

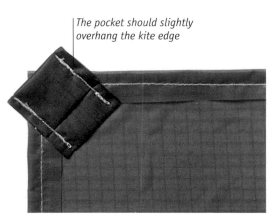

3 Fold in the longer end to create a pocket. Sew along the pocket sides to seal them.

MAKING TABS

Tabs are short strips of fabric, doubled over and sewn to the cover to house line.

1 Cut a strip of nylon 2.5 cm (1 in) wide; allow 5 cm (2 in) in length for each tab.

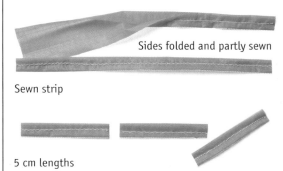

Sides folded and partly sewn

Sewn strip

5 cm lengths

2 Fold in the two long sides so that the strip is a third of its original width. Sew the strip down the centre over the folded sides, and cut into 5 cm (2 in) lengths.

MAKING REINFORCING PATCHES

These triangular patches strengthen a hole so that it does not give when you insert a spar. Stick the patch down first, then cut the hole.

Tape stuck on nylon

Nylon-backed tape

1 Cut a length of double-sided carpet tape, allowing 5 cm (2 in) for each pair of patches, and stick it to a scrap of nylon. Trim the nylon around the tape.

5 cm length

Triangular patches

Hole cut in reinforcing patch

Patch stuck in place

2 Cut the tape into 5 cm (2 in) lengths and cut each length in half diagonally. Peel off the backing and stick the patch in position on the kite. Cut a hole in the patch to insert the spar.

CUTTING A HOLE

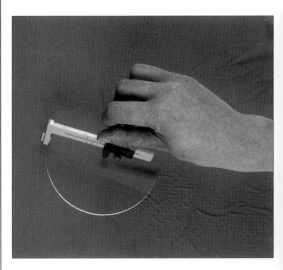

It is best to use a circle cutter to cut a hole, although you can draw the circle with a pair of compasses and cut it out with scissors, or even use a soldering iron and template. Put the point of the cutter in the centre of where you want the hole to be, adjust the cutter to the right diameter, then cut the hole.

HOT-CUTTING FABRIC

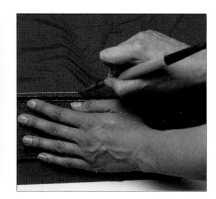

Use a soldering iron to hot-cut nylon or webbing and stop the edges from fraying. When the iron has heated up, hold the handle like a pen and carefully trace the point along a straight edge or template.

WARNINGS
▲ When hot-cutting, make sure that the room is well ventilated as the material gives off fumes.
▲ Take care not to burn your fingers when heat-sealing line.

HEAT-SEALING LINE
Use matches, a lighter or a soldering iron to melt the ends of line and stop them fraying.

PREPARING DOWEL

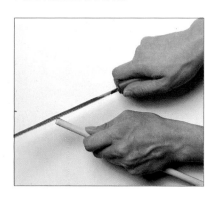

1 Cut the dowel to length with a small hacksaw and use a file to round the ends.

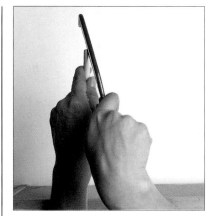

2 If you need to make a notch in the ends to house loops of line, saw to a depth of 5 mm (¼ in) halfway across each end.

JOINING SPARS AT AN ANGLE

1 Cut a piece of plastic tube 3-8 cm (1¼-3 in) long, depending on the diameter of the spar, and midway along cut a slot with a pair of scissors halfway across its width.

2 Make another cut at a 45° angle to the first to create a wedge shape. Bend the tube down at the wedge to angle it and insert the spars.

Fitting the spars

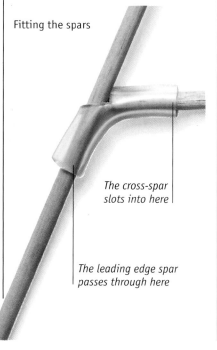

The cross-spar slots into here

The leading edge spar passes through here

TYING KNOTS

These are the basic knots in kite-making. The overhand and slip knots are mainly used in constructing a kite. The lark's head knot attaches the ring to the bridle and is easily moved to adjust the flight angle. The bowline knot is good for tying the flying line to the bridle ring.

OVERHAND KNOT

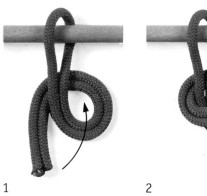

1   2   3

SLIP KNOT

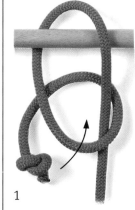

1   2   3

BOWLINE KNOT

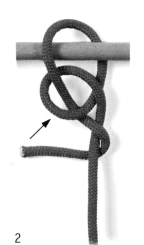

1   2   3

LARK'S HEAD KNOT

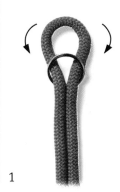

1   2   3

65

SIMPLE SLED

One of the easiest kites to make, this sled involves little more than hemming the nylon, sewing sleeves to hold the spars on each side and hot-cutting two vents. Designed for light to moderate winds, the kite is flown on line with a breaking strain of 25-32 kg (50-70 lb). If the sled does not fly perfectly straight, move the bridle ring away from the direction the kite favours.

MATERIALS & EQUIPMENT

▲ 1 m (3 ft) ripstop nylon
▲ 2.5 m (8 ft) of 25 kg (50 lb) braided nylon line
▲ One aluminium ring
▲ Two 88 cm (35 in) lengths of 6 mm (¼ in) ramin dowel
▲ Flying line

▲ Pen or tailor's chalk
▲ Ruler/set square
▲ Scissors
▲ Pins
▲ Sewing machine and thread
▲ Matches or lighter
▲ Soldering iron
▲ Plate (diameter approx. 18 cm [7 in])
▲ File

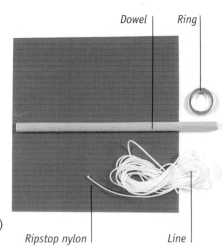

Dowel Ring

Ripstop nylon   Line

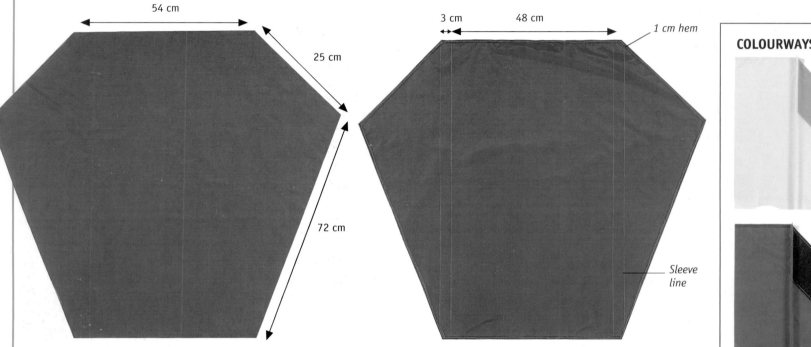

1 Following the cutting pattern, mark and cut out the ripstop nylon.

54 cm
25 cm
72 cm

3 cm 48 cm 1 cm hem

Sleeve line

2 Fold over, pin and sew a 1 cm (½ in) hem around the edge of the cover. Draw the sleeve lines and turn the fabric over so that the lines face down.

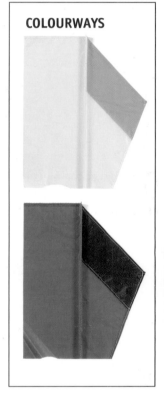

COLOURWAYS

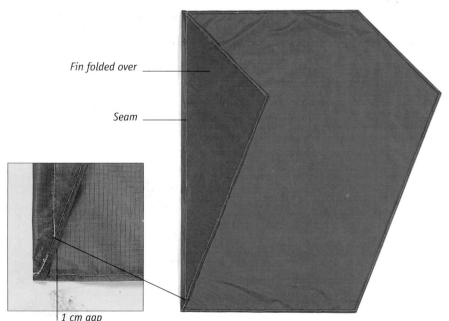

Fin folded over

Seam

1 cm gap

3 Fold over a fin so that the sleeve lines are together. Seam the sleeve, sewing across both ends and leaving a 1 cm (½ in) gap, 1 cm (½ in) from the bottom. Repeat with the other fin.

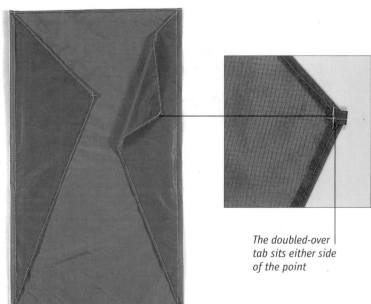

The doubled-over tab sits either side of the point

4 Make two tabs from scrap ripstop nylon and stitch to the points of the fins.

WARNINGS
▲ When hot-cutting, make sure that the room is well ventilated as nylon gives off harmful fumes.
▲ Do not touch the point of the soldering iron as this becomes very hot and can burn even after the iron has been unplugged.

The legs of the bridle should be the same length

6 Using a soldering iron and the plate as a template, hot-cut two circles 15 cm (6 in) from the bottom of the kite. These form the vents.

5 Heat-seal the ends of the line. Tie one end to each tab and using a lark's head knot, attach the ring at the line midpoint.

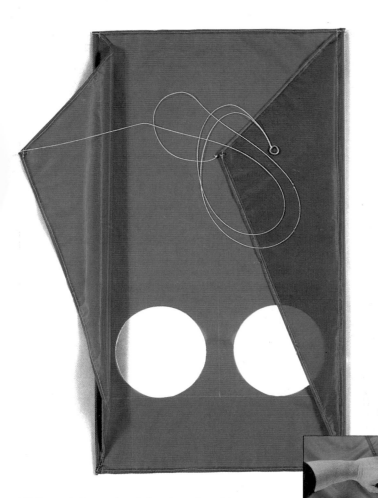

7 Round the ends of the dowel and insert each length into a sleeve through a gap. The spars should fit tightly without distortion. Tie the flying line to the ring.

Shaped by the wind
In flight, the wind billows out the cover and gives it a curved shape. The vents add stability.

TECHNIQUES
See pages 64-5

Making tabs

Heat-sealing

Lark's head knot

Hot-cutting

Preparing dowel

DELLA PORTA

Basically just a rectangle of fabric with two diagonal spars, four pockets and a long loop tail, the classic Della Porta is simple to make. To vary the look, appliqué the cover or make it from bands of different-coloured ripstop nylon sewn together. The kite is very stable in a wide range of winds. It should be flown on line with a breaking strain of 12 kg (25 lb).

MATERIALS & EQUIPMENT

▲ 1.15 m (3¾ ft) ripstop nylon
▲ Two 80 cm (31½ in) lengths of 6 mm (¼ in) ramin dowel
▲ About 2.2 m (7 ft) of 25 kg (50 lb) braided nylon line
▲ One aluminium ring
▲ Flying line

▲ Pen or tailor's chalk
▲ Ruler/set square
▲ Scissors
▲ Pins
▲ Sewing machine and thread
▲ File
▲ Matches or lighter
▲ Wide-eyed needle

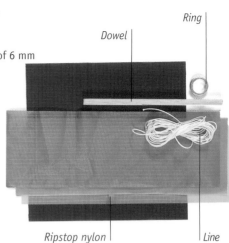

Ring

Dowel

Ripstop nylon

Line

MAKING THE COVER

1 Following the cutting pattern, mark and cut out the nylon.

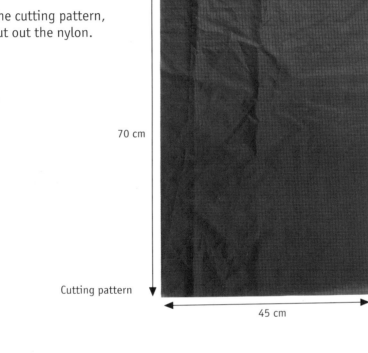

70 cm

Cutting pattern

45 cm

1.05

10 cm

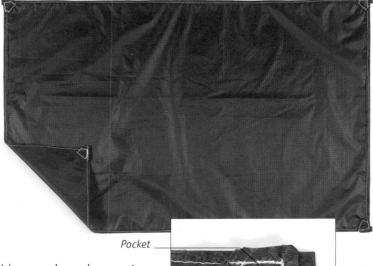

Pocket

Tab

1 cm hem

2 Fold over, pin and sew a 1 cm (½ in) hem around the edge of the rectangle. Make six tabs and four pockets and sew one of each on to every corner of the wrong side of the rectangle.

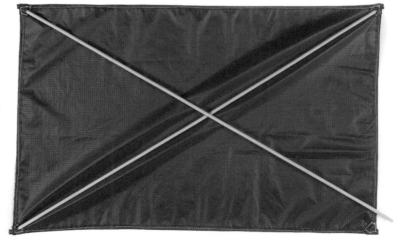

3 Round the ends of the dowel and insert the lengths diagonally into the pockets. The sticks should fit tightly without distorting themselves or the cover of the kite.

ATTACHING THE BRIDLE

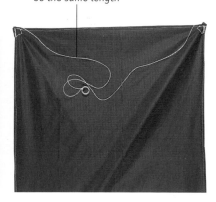

The legs of the bridle should be the same length

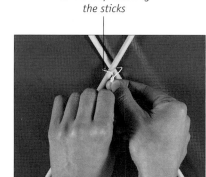

Centre loop securing the sticks

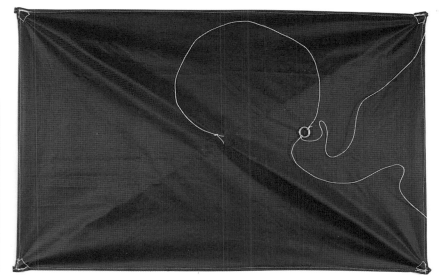

1 Cut the line into a 1 m (3 ft) length, a 62 cm (24½ in) length and three 15 cm (6 in) lengths, and heat-seal the ends. Tie the ring with a lark's head knot halfway along the 1 m (3 ft) length, then tie each end to the tabs at the top corners of the kite.

2 Use a wide-eyed needle to thread a 15 cm (6 in) length through to the front of the kite on one side of the crossed sticks. Bring the length up again to the back on the other side of the sticks. Tie an overhand knot to create a small loop.

3 Pull the loop through to the front and using slip knots, tie one end of the 62 cm (24½ in) length to the centre loop and the other end to the ring. Tie the flying line to the ring.

ADDING A TAIL

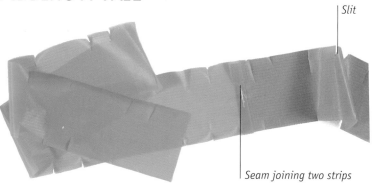

Slit

Seam joining two strips

1 Sew the strips of ripstop together end to end to make a tail, and cut slits randomly in both sides.

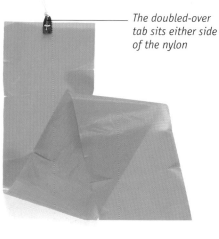

The doubled-over tab sits either side of the nylon

2 Sew a tab to each tail end. Thread a 15 cm (6 in) length of line through each tab, line up the ends and tie an overhand knot near the tab. Tie the tail to the tabs at the bottom corners.

Stable in flight
Once the kite is airborne, the long loop tail keeps it on a straight course if it wanders to one side.

TECHNIQUES
See pages 64-5

Making tabs

Making a pocket

Preparing dowel

Heat-sealing

Lark's head knot

Overhand knot

Slip knot

SIX-PACK

A six-celled soft kite based on the sled design, the Six-pack flies at a very high angle and in a wide range of winds. It is fairly simple to make because of its lack of spars and needs no assembly. The fins on the cover are a contrasting colour; for a different effect, add a third colour into the design, or make a kite of one colour. The Six-pack should be flown with a drogue and on line with a breaking strain of 12-25 kg (25-50 lb).

MATERIALS & EQUIPMENT

▲ 2 m (6½ ft) ripstop nylon
▲ 12 m (40 ft) of 25 kg (50 lb) braided nylon line
▲ Two aluminium rings
▲ One swivel clip

▲ Pen or tailor's chalk
▲ Ruler/set square
▲ Scissors
▲ Sewing machine and thread
▲ Pins
▲ Matches or lighter
▲ Wide-eyed needle

Ripstop nylon

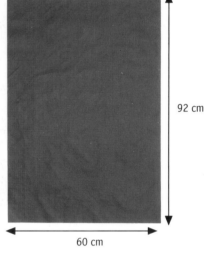

Line

Ring

Swivel clip

MAKING THE COVER

1 Following the cutting pattern, mark and cut out two rectangles, four triangles and the cone-shaped drogue pieces from the nylon.

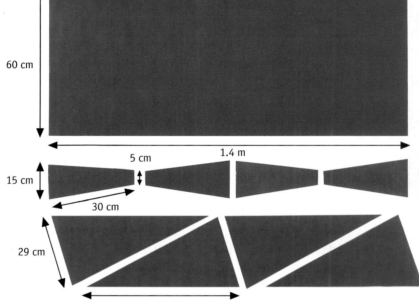

Cutting pattern

60 cm

92 cm

60 cm

15 cm

5 cm

1.4 m

30 cm

29 cm

61 cm

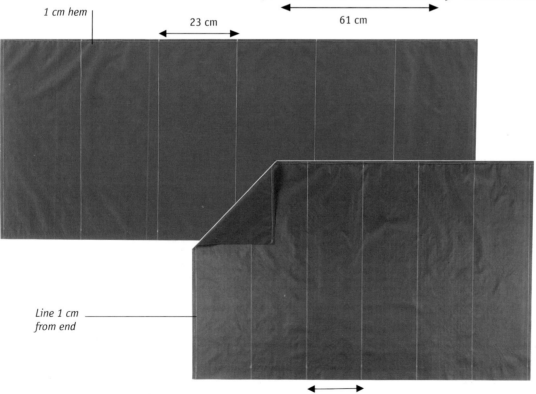

1 cm hem

23 cm

Line 1 cm from end

15 cm

Tab

1 cm hem

2 Fold over and sew a 1 cm (½ in) hem along one long edge of each rectangle. Draw a line 1 cm (½ in) in from each end of the rectangles, and mark the space between the lines into six equal sections as shown.

3 To make the fins, sew a 1 cm (½ in) hem along two sides - one long and one short - of the triangles. Stitch a tab to the point between the hemmed sides.

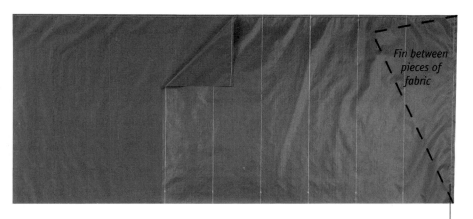

Fin between pieces of fabric

Seam 1 cm from edge

4 Place the rectangles with right sides facing and one end of each together. Put a fin between the two and pin. Sew 1 cm (½ in) in from the edge.

5 Repeat with the other end, aligning the edges of the rectangles and sewing another fin between the two.

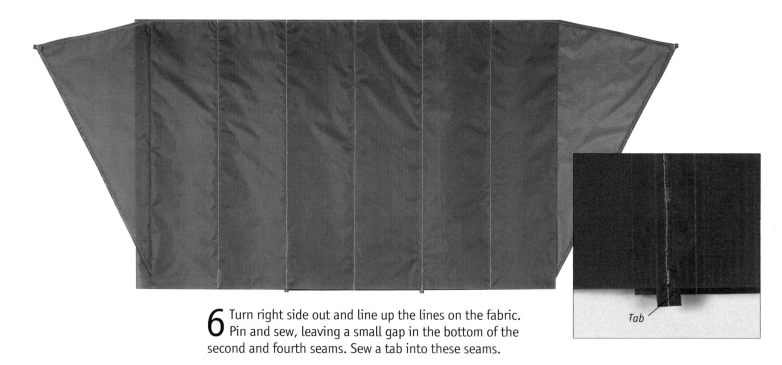

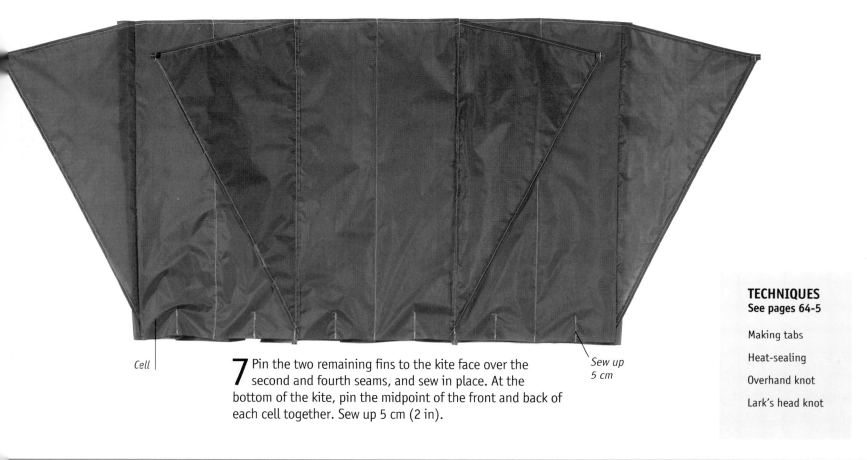

Tab

6 Turn right side out and line up the lines on the fabric. Pin and sew, leaving a small gap in the bottom of the second and fourth seams. Sew a tab into these seams.

Cell

Sew up 5 cm

7 Pin the two remaining fins to the kite face over the second and fourth seams, and sew in place. At the bottom of the kite, pin the midpoint of the front and back of each cell together. Sew up 5 cm (2 in).

TECHNIQUES
See pages 64-5

Making tabs

Heat-sealing

Overhand knot

Lark's head knot

ATTACHING THE BRIDLE

1 Cut two 3 m (10 ft) lengths of 25 kg (50 lb) line and heat-seal the ends. Thread the lengths through a ring and line up the ends. Tie an overhand knot near the ring. Then, tie one end to each fin tab.

2 Cut a 50 cm (20 in) length of 25 kg (50 lb) line and heat-seal the ends. Tie one end to each tab at the bottom of the kite. Using a lark's head knot, tie the other ring at the midpoint of this line.

ADDING A DROGUE

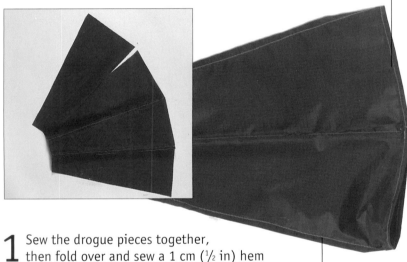

1 cm hem

Seam joining two drogue pieces

1 Sew the drogue pieces together, then fold over and sew a 1 cm (½ in) hem around the top (the wider part). With the seams outside, sew the last two sides together to make a tube. Turn right side out.

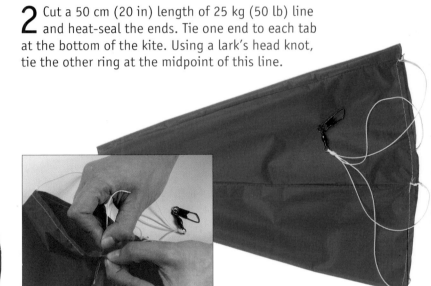

Make sure that the lines are the same length

2 Cut two 50 cm (20 in) lengths of 25 kg (50 lb) line and heat-seal the ends. Thread the lengths through the loop on the bottom of the swivel clip and line up the ends. Tie an overhand knot near the loop. Use a needle to thread one end through the top of a seam joining two drogue pieces and tie off. Repeat with the other ends.

3 Take the last length of 25 kg (50 lb) line and tie one end to the ring on the bottom of the kite. Tie an overhand knot to create a loop in the other end, and clip on the drogue. Tie the flying line to the bridle ring.

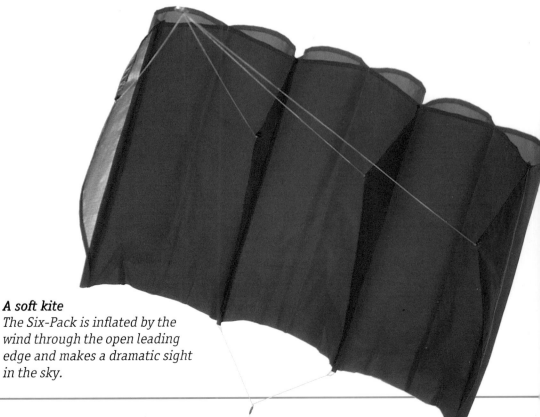

A soft kite
The Six-Pack is inflated by the wind through the open leading edge and makes a dramatic sight in the sky.

TUMBLING STAR

A multi-faceted, single-celled box kite, the Tumbling Star is great fun to fly as it rolls and tumbles in light to moderate winds. Making the six-pointed Star is not as complicated as it looks because many of the steps are repetitive. Choose different colours of ripstop nylon for the central section and the points on the Star so that they alternate as the kite tumbles. Fly the Star on line with a breaking strain of 25 kg (50 lb).

MATERIALS & EQUIPMENT

▲ 1.6 m (5¼ ft) ripstop nylon
▲ 2.5 m (8 ft) of 25 kg (50 lb) braided nylon line
▲ Six 29 cm (11½ in) lengths of 6 mm (¼ in) ramin dowel
▲ Three 1.05 m (3½ ft) lengths of 6 mm (¼ in) ramin dowel
▲ One aluminium ring
▲ Flying line

▲ Pen or tailor's chalk
▲ Ruler/set square
▲ Scissors
▲ Sewing machine and thread
▲ Circle cutter
▲ Pins
▲ Matches or lighter
▲ File
▲ Hacksaw

Dowel
Ripstop nylon
Line   *Ring*

MAKING THE CENTRAL SECTION

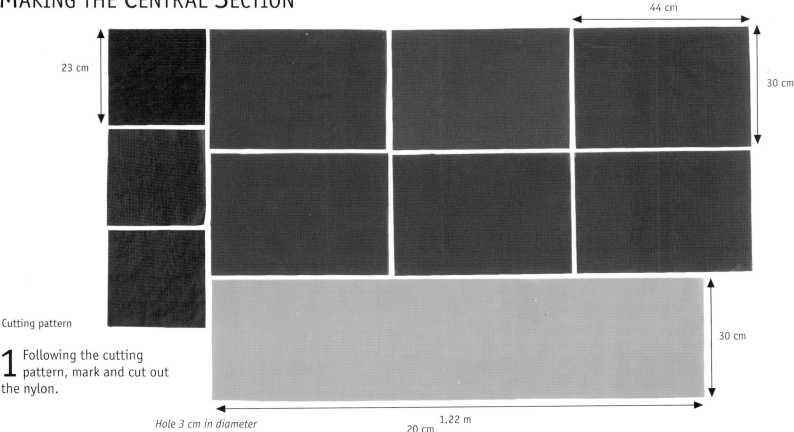

23 cm

44 cm

30 cm

30 cm

Cutting pattern

1 Following the cutting pattern, mark and cut out the nylon.

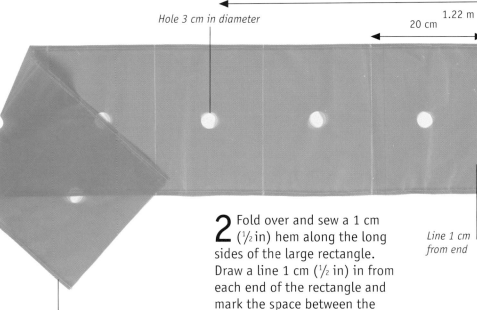

Hole 3 cm in diameter

20 cm

1.22 m

1 cm hem

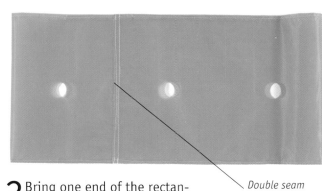

Line 1 cm from end

Double seam for extra strength

2 Fold over and sew a 1 cm (½ in) hem along the long sides of the large rectangle. Draw a line 1 cm (½ in) in from each end of the rectangle and mark the space between the lines into six equal sections. Cut a circular hole in the centre of each section.

3 Bring one end of the rectangle over to line up with the other end, right sides together. Sew together 1 cm (½ in) from the edge. Fold this seam down to one side so that it lies flat, and sew. Turn right side out.

ADDING THE POINTS

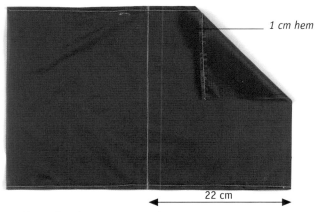

1 cm hem

22 cm

1 To make the outer panels, sew a 1 cm (½ in) hem along the long sides of each small rectangle. Mark into two equal sections.

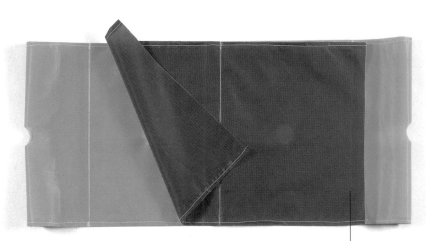

Right side of fabric

2 Join the panels to the central section, aligning the line on each panel with a section line. Pin and sew.

3 Pin the end of one panel to the end of the next. Sew 2 cm (¾ in) in from the edge, leaving a 1 cm (½ in) gap in the seam at one end. Repeat with the other panels.

1 cm gap

Seam

MAKING THE WINGS

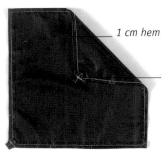

1 cm hem

The doubled-over tab sits either side of the corner

1 Fold over, pin and sew a 1 cm (½ in) hem around the edge of each square. Make nine tabs and stitch a tab to two opposite corners of the squares.

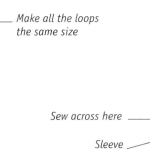

Make all the loops the same size

2 Cut six 10 cm (4 in) lengths of 25 kg (50 lb) line and heat-seal the ends. Thread a length through a tab and tie an overhand knot to make a loop. Repeat with the other lengths. Cut the squares in half diagonally to create two triangles.

Sew across here

Sleeve

3 Put a wing between the flaps where the end of one panel meets another. Pin across the top of the flaps, and sew. Then sew down the ends of the flaps to make an enclosed sleeve.

The end with the tabs becomes the front

4 Repeat with the other wings, making sure that they all face the same way, sewing a tab into the same end of every other sleeve, as you seal the ends.

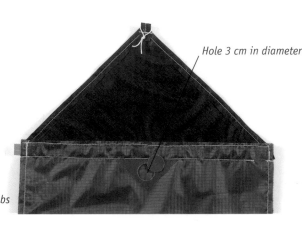

Hole 3 cm in diameter

5 Stick a reinforcing patch below a sleeve halfway across the same side of each point. Cut holes through the patches.

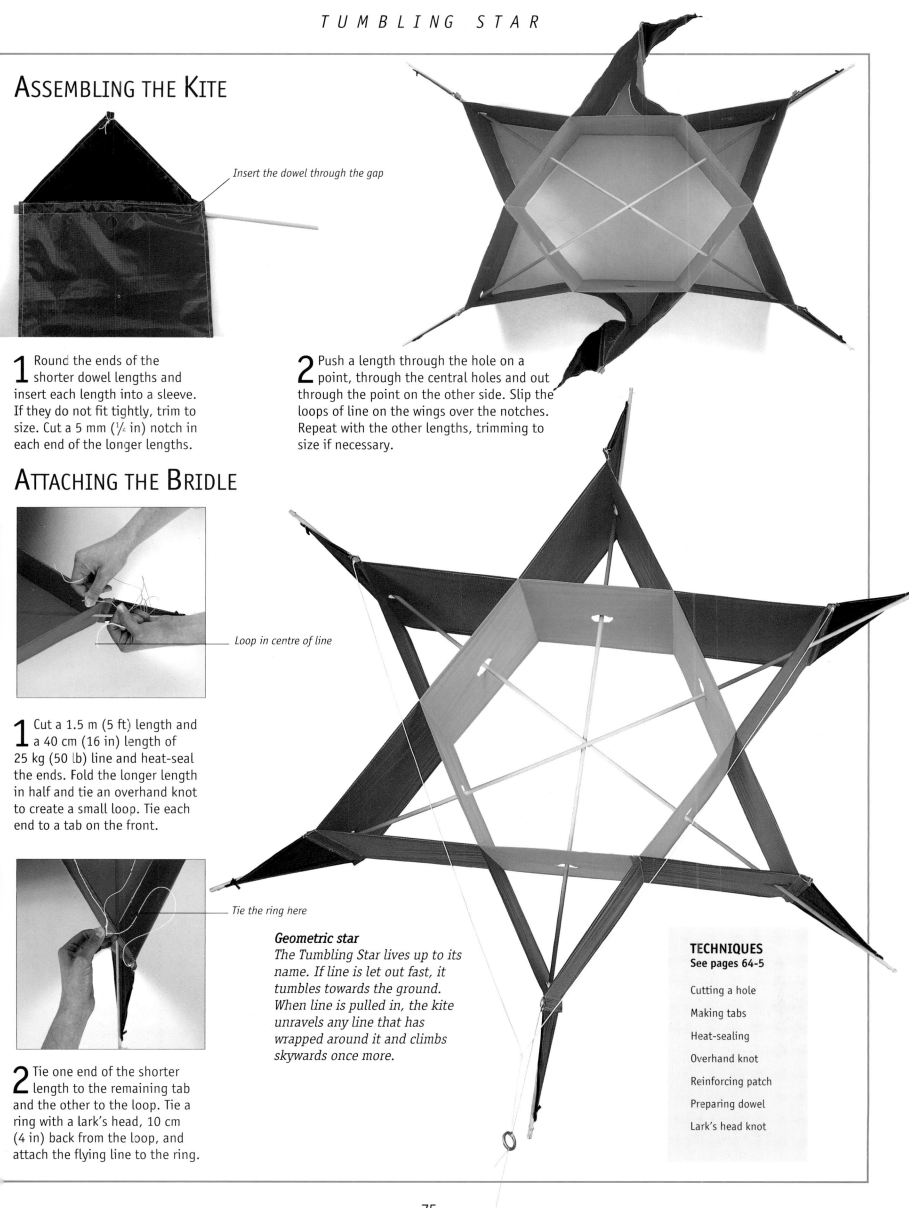

ASSEMBLING THE KITE

Insert the dowel through the gap

1 Round the ends of the shorter dowel lengths and insert each length into a sleeve. If they do not fit tightly, trim to size. Cut a 5 mm (¼ in) notch in each end of the longer lengths.

2 Push a length through the hole on a point, through the central holes and out through the point on the other side. Slip the loops of line on the wings over the notches. Repeat with the other lengths, trimming to size if necessary.

ATTACHING THE BRIDLE

Loop in centre of line

1 Cut a 1.5 m (5 ft) length and a 40 cm (16 in) length of 25 kg (50 lb) line and heat-seal the ends. Fold the longer length in half and tie an overhand knot to create a small loop. Tie each end to a tab on the front.

Tie the ring here

2 Tie one end of the shorter length to the remaining tab and the other to the loop. Tie a ring with a lark's head, 10 cm (4 in) back from the loop, and attach the flying line to the ring.

Geometric star
The Tumbling Star lives up to its name. If line is let out fast, it tumbles towards the ground. When line is pulled in, the kite unravels any line that has wrapped around it and climbs skywards once more.

TECHNIQUES
See pages 64-5

Cutting a hole

Making tabs

Heat-sealing

Overhand knot

Reinforcing patch

Preparing dowel

Lark's head knot

STUNTER

This highly manoeuvrable stunt kite combines a streamlined delta shape with the simple construction of a fighter. Made in two halves, which are then joined together, the stunter has only a flexible bow and a spine for its framework. Once airborne, the kite can perform all the basic stunt manoeuvres, from looping the loop to describing squares and figures of eight. Fly the stunter on line with a breaking strain of 18 kg (40 lb).

MATERIALS & EQUIPMENT

▲ 80 cm (31½ in) ripstop nylon
▲ One 58 cm (23 in) length and one 1.7 m (5½ ft) length of 4 mm (¼ in) fibreglass rod
▲ About 1.9 m (6 ft) of 25 kg (50 lb) braided nylon line
▲ Two aluminium rings
▲ Two 30 m (100 ft) lengths of flying line

▲ Pen or tailor's chalk
▲ Ruler/set square
▲ Scissors
▲ Sewing machine and thread
▲ Matches or lighter
▲ Wide-eyed needle

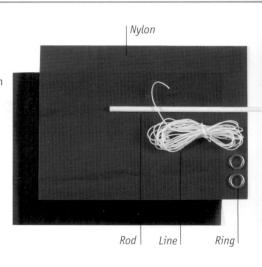

Nylon

Rod *Line* *Ring*

MAKING THE COVER

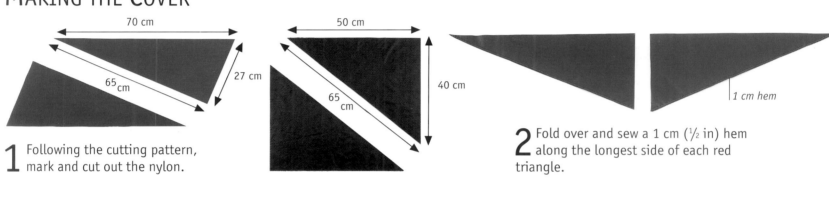

70 cm
65 cm
27 cm

50 cm
65 cm
40 cm

1 cm hem

1 Following the cutting pattern, mark and cut out the nylon.

2 Fold over and sew a 1 cm (½ in) hem along the longest side of each red triangle.

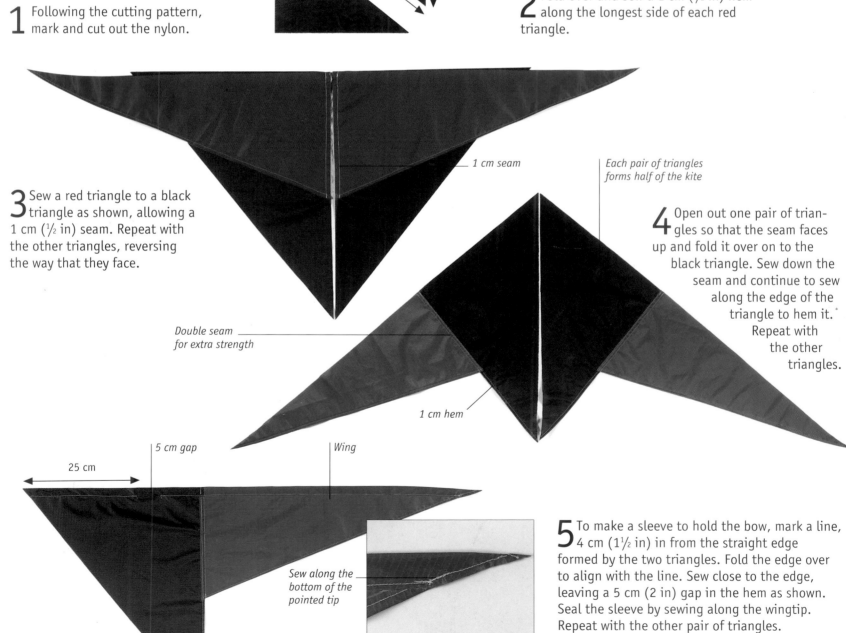

1 cm seam

Each pair of triangles forms half of the kite

3 Sew a red triangle to a black triangle as shown, allowing a 1 cm (½ in) seam. Repeat with the other triangles, reversing the way that they face.

Double seam for extra strength

1 cm hem

4 Open out one pair of triangles so that the seam faces up and fold it over on to the black triangle. Sew down the seam and continue to sew along the edge of the triangle to hem it. Repeat with the other triangles.

5 cm gap

Wing

25 cm

Sew along the bottom of the pointed tip

5 To make a sleeve to hold the bow, mark a line, 4 cm (1½ in) in from the straight edge formed by the two triangles. Fold the edge over to align with the line. Sew close to the edge, leaving a 5 cm (2 in) gap in the hem as shown. Seal the sleeve by sewing along the wingtip. Repeat with the other pair of triangles.

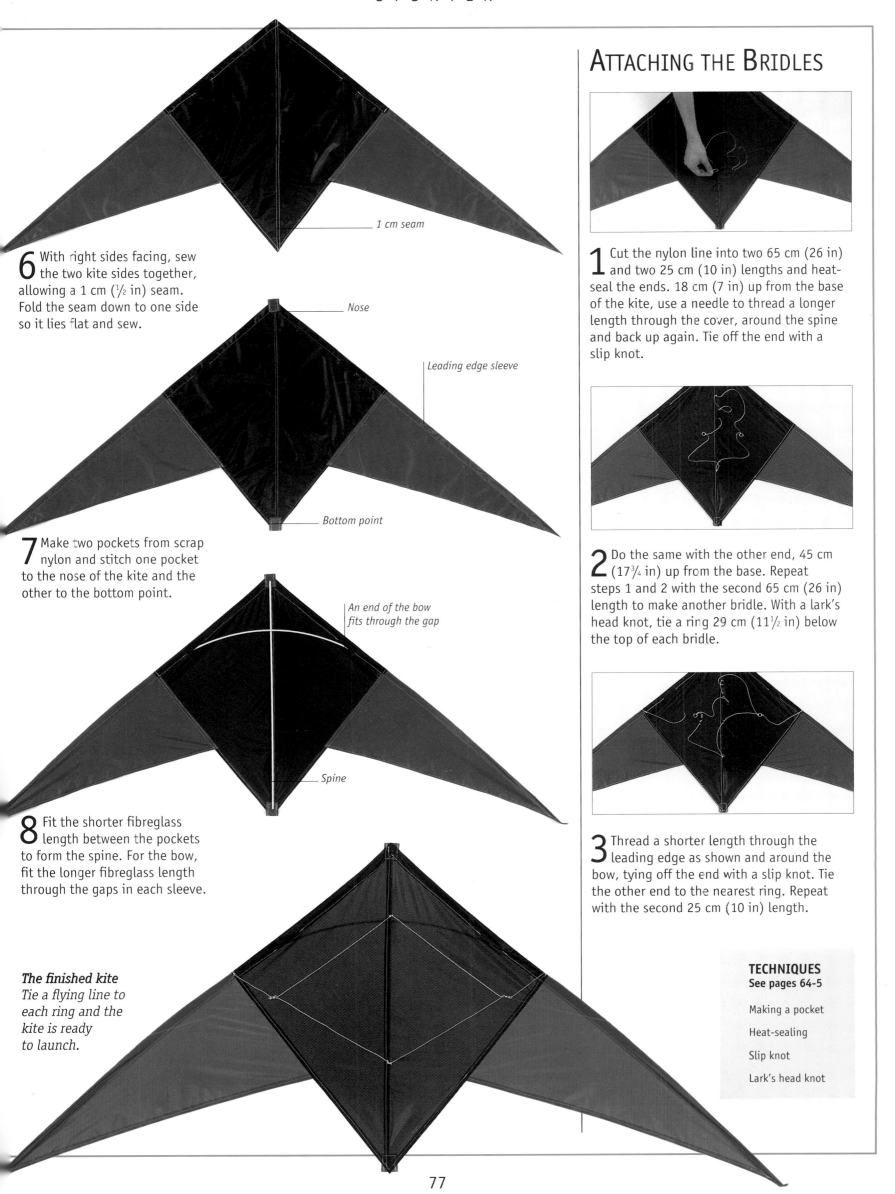

ATTACHING THE BRIDLES

6 With right sides facing, sew the two kite sides together, allowing a 1 cm (½ in) seam. Fold the seam down to one side so it lies flat and sew.

1 cm seam

7 Make two pockets from scrap nylon and stitch one pocket to the nose of the kite and the other to the bottom point.

Nose

Leading edge sleeve

Bottom point

8 Fit the shorter fibreglass length between the pockets to form the spine. For the bow, fit the longer fibreglass length through the gaps in each sleeve.

An end of the bow fits through the gap

Spine

The finished kite
Tie a flying line to each ring and the kite is ready to launch.

1 Cut the nylon line into two 65 cm (26 in) and two 25 cm (10 in) lengths and heat-seal the ends. 18 cm (7 in) up from the base of the kite, use a needle to thread a longer length through the cover, around the spine and back up again. Tie off the end with a slip knot.

2 Do the same with the other end, 45 cm (17¾ in) up from the base. Repeat steps 1 and 2 with the second 65 cm (26 in) length to make another bridle. With a lark's head knot, tie a ring 29 cm (11½ in) below the top of each bridle.

3 Thread a shorter length through the leading edge as shown and around the bow, tying off the end with a slip knot. Tie the other end to the nearest ring. Repeat with the second 25 cm (10 in) length.

TECHNIQUES
See pages 64-5

Making a pocket

Heat-sealing

Slip knot

Lark's head knot

SUPPLIERS & ORGANIZATIONS

GREAT BRITAIN

The Kite Store
48 Neal Street
London WC2H 9PA
Tel: 071-836-1666

Sky Bums
Victorian Arcade
Shrewsbury SY1 1PU
Tel: 0743-244677

Bristol Kite Store
1b Pitville Place
Cotham Hill
Bristol BS6 6JY
Tel: 0272-745010

High Flyers
The Kite Site
The Mowhay
Trebetherick
Wadebridge
Cornwall PL27 6SE
Tel: 0208-62567

Windthings
11 Cowgatehead
Edinburgh EH1 1JY
Tel: 031-220-6336

Kite Society of Great Britain
31 Grange Road
Ilford
Essex IG1 1EU

STACK (Stunt, Team and
Competitive Kiting)
Tony Cartwright
78 Dongola Road
London N17 6EE

UNITED STATES

Windborne Kites
585 Cannery Row #105
Monterey CA 93940
Tel: 408-373-7422

Catch the Wind
266 S.E. Highway 101
Lincoln City OR 97367
Tel: 800-227-7878

Kligs Kites
Galleria
9600 N. Kings Highway
Myrtle Beach SC 29577
Tel: 800-333-5944

Into the Wind
1408 Pearl Street
Boulder CO 80302
Tel: 303-449-5356

Kite Loft
511 Broadwalk
Ocean City MD 21842
Tel: 301-289-7855

American Kite Flyers' Assoc.
1559 Rockville Pike
Rockville MD 20852

CANADA

Touch the Sky - Harbourside
Queen's Quay Terminal
207 Queen's Quay West
Toronto, Ontario
M5J 1A7
Tel: 416-362-5983

Touch the Sky Inc.
21 Goodrich Road
Unit 6
Toronto, Ontario
M8T 6A3
Tel: 416-252-3200

Paint the Sky Kite Company
Station Mall
293 Bay Street
Sault Ste. Marie, Ontario
P6A 1X3
Tel: 705-945-7948

AUSTRALIA

Breeze & Eeze Pty Ltd
Harbourside Festival Marketplace
Darling Harbour NSW 2000
Tel: 02-281-4348

Highly Strung Kites
51 Glenhuntly Road
Elwood Vic 3184
Tel: 03-531-3630

Windworks Kite Co.
The Wharf
Parkyn Parade
Mooloolaba QLD 4557
Tel: 074-448-482

The Kite Shop
95 Kingston Avenue
Dawe Park SA 5041
Tel: 08-276-1740

Hold the line
357 Cambridge Street
Wembley WA
Tel: 09-387-5676

Australian Kite Flyers' Assoc.
PO Box 110
Sylvania Southgate NSW 2224
Tel: 02-521-7631

GERMANY

Wolkensturmer
Hansastrasse 52
D2000 Hamburg 13
Tel: 040-45-49-71

Vom Winde Verweht
Eisenacherstrasse 81
D1000 Berlin 62
Tel: 030-784-7769

Drachen Dompteur
Alt Nied 4-8
6000 Frankfurt Nied
Tel: 069-38-20-21

Zieh Leine Drachenladen
Ellerstrasse 134
D4000 Düsseldorf 1
Tel: 0211-78-35-83

THE NETHERLANDS

Vlieger OP
Weteringkade 5-A
2515-AK Den Haag
Tel: 70-85-85-86

AUSTRIA

Fly High Drachen
Argentinierstrasse 16
A-1040 Wien
Tel: 222-505-0260

ACKNOWLEDGMENTS

Authors' acknowledgments: We would like to thank the following people for their invaluable help during the writing of this book: Andy King and Viv Walters from the Kite Store for lending kites for photoshoots and giving us support, Sarah Kent for her input and modelling in the Flying Kites section, Gill and Jon Bloom for going over final text, and Tim Walker for photographing us at short notice.

Thanks to our editor, Tanya Hines, whose skill and tireless efforts have brought the whole book together, and Daphne Razazan for her guidance, especially during the early stages of the project. To Nigel Osborne and Matthew Chattle for their design and photographic skills.

We are grateful to the following for the use of their kites: The Kite Store, Martin Lester, Windy Kites, Joel Scholz, High Flyers, Peter Lynn, Top of the Line, Tony Slater, Raindrop Kites, Graham Wyle, Wolfgang Schimmelpfennig, Rare Air Kites, John Barker (parachuting teddy).

Dorling Kindersley would like to thank The Kite Store for loaning kites for photography, Sarah Kent for her expertise and modelling in the book, Gill and Jon Bloom for checking proofs, and Andy Smith for help on the aerodynamics section. Thanks also to Mark Thomson for computer page layouts and Hilary Bird for the index.

Photographic credits
All photographs by Matthew Chattle except:
Barnaby's Picture Library, Robin Dawson: p.1; Gill and Jon Bloom: pp.8-9; Paul Bricknell: pp.34, 36c, 36-7 (main pic); Martin Cameron: pp.44, 45 (all pix except tl & box kite), 46-7 (main pic); Sarah Kent: pp.17bl, 35tr, 46t; Pictor International: pp.42-3; Susanna Price: pp.14t, 21tr, 24 (boxed pic), 32l, 33, 37tr, 43 (inset), 46b, 59 (inset); Anne Ronan Picture Library: pp.10, 11tl; Royal Aeronautical Society: p.11tr; Tim Walker: p.6
Key: t = top; b = bottom; c = centre; l = left; r = right